# Math Conundrums

## Dynamic Learning Adventures

by Marjorie Frank

Illustrated by Kathleen Bullock

Incentive Publications, Inc.
Nashville, Tennessee

# To Teachers and Parents

- Use each math conundrum as a short warm-up to stimulate math reasoning and build excitement about what math can do, OR as the basis for a longer math lesson focused on the related skills.

- Use all the conundrums randomly. Or choose a conundrum that specifically fits a skill or standard—to introduce, review, or sharpen that skill.

- Let students work alone or in pairs on the conundrums, OR use them with the whole group.

- The math conundrums can be used as take-home challenge problems. Give the students a few days to ponder the conundrum and bring a solution to share and compare.

- Help students identify the strategy or strategies used for each conundrum. Note that different strategies may be applied to the same problem. Compare problem-solving approaches. Ask students to explain how they arrived at their solutions.

- Help students connect the concepts and processes to their real lives. Ask them to think of places and times they have used or might use the same problem-solving strategy.

- Help students connect with the cartoons and comic strips so that they can create their own math conundrums inspired by the antics of Rosco and his friends.

- The skills covered are applicable to courses in general math, pre-algebra, or algebra.

- See pages 5 to 8 for lists of skills and standards supported by this program, 100 to 105 for a cumulative assessment, and 107 to 108 for an alphabetical list of the words with meanings and pronunciations.

*Illustrated by Kathleen Bullock*
*Cover design by Debbie Weekly*
*Edited by Joy MacKenzie*

ISBN 978-0-86530-526-7

What do you get when you mix the antics of a clever street-smart rat with dozens of clever math problems? You get unique challenges that put your math skills to good use—plus a whole lot of adventuresome fun!

# Math to Stretch Your Brain

Join Rosco Rat and his band of independent (and slightly quirky) friends as they find themselves in all sorts of dilemmas.

- To handle these dilemmas, the friends (and you) will need to use a host of problem-solving strategies.

- They (and you) must be quick and flexible in using many reasoning skills, as well as plenty of wit and wisdom.

- Each conundrum invites you to apply endless ingenuity and all your best math knowledge to conventional and unconventional (but sensible) everyday problems.

- The book is full of surprises, humor, delightful cartoons, and intrigue. It will leave you with the gift of sharper thinking skills and a lot more excitement about the wonder and fun of math.

## CONTENTS

### Appendix

## *To the Student:*
# Untangle These Conundrums!

A conundrum is a complicated and difficult problem. These math conundrums are questions or situations that will surprise, puzzle, stretch, and delight you. To solve them, you will put to use many thinking skills and much math knowledge that you already have.

- Take on these math challenges in any order. Choose the ones that you think you can do.

- Don't shy away from those that look trickier, though. Take the chance and let them stretch your mind!

- Read each conundrum carefully—twice. Make sure you clearly identify the problem. (What, exactly, are you asked to do or find?)

- You can tackle a conundrum alone, but sometimes it is fun to work with a partner or small group.

- If you are having trouble with one of the problems, ask someone to join you on pondering the problem.

- Think about the strategy you are using as you try to solve each conundrum. If one strategy is not working well, try a different approach.

- It is always a good idea to explain ahead of time what your plan is for solving the problem. You can tell this to someone else or write it down.

- When you find a solution, explain how you found it. Go back through the steps you followed.

- Compare your solutions and strategies with someone else.

- Try not to look at the answers too soon. If you are stuck, have someone else peek at the answer and give you a hint.

- When you do reach a solution, choose another strategy to check your answer.

- All of these conundrums will push you to think creatively and push your math understandings to their limits. Have fun with Rosco and his crazy conundrums!

- When you have time, create some of your own conundrums about Rosco and his friends—or about you and your friends!

# Math Standards and Skills Supported by the Conundrums

| Skill | Conundrum Number(s) |
|---|---|
| Make use of number concepts, systems, and relationships; order and compare numbers | 4, 30, 33, 39, 40, 47, 53, 62, 63, 70, 80, 82, 87, 88 |
| Evaluate expressions, including those with roots, radicals, exponential numbers, and scientific notation | 7, 17, 29, 42, 43, 63, 73, 77 |
| Perform operations with whole numbers and integers | 1, 3, 5, 11, 13, 15, 19, 27, 29, 30, 31, 34, 39, 41, 45, 60, 63, 66, 67, 70, 72, 73, 74, 79, 85, 89 |
| Perform operations with rational numbers | 1, 3, 4, 8, 9, 14, 17, 21, 22, 28, 30, 40, 43, 45, 49, 55, 57, 62, 63, 71, 80, 81, 86, 88, 90 |
| Find rate, ratios, proportions, and percents | 9, 17, 22, 25, 26, 30, 37, 38, 44, 47, 49, 51, 55, 56, 57, 63, 71, 79, 81, 86, 87, 89 |
| Use geometry, measurement, and formulas to solve problems | 1, 6, 8, 11, 12, 14, 18, 21, 26, 33, 34, 40, 45, 47, 58, 59, 60, 62, 68, 72, 76, 83, 84, 86 |
| Use the Pythagorean theorem to solve problems | 34, 68 |
| Solve time problems | 1, 11, 16, 30, 59, 74, 81, 90 |
| Solve money problems | 5, 32, 70, 79, 80, 81 |
| Use algebraic relationships to solve problems | 3, 7, 9, 11, 13, 14, 17, 19, 27, 29, 39, 42, 43, 44, 52, 55, 56, 63, 64, 65, 68, 71, 76, 77, 79, 81, 89 |
| Solve equations | 2, 9, 11, 12, 15, 17, 19, 22, 25, 26, 28, 29, 30, 31, 33, 34, 37, 38, 40, 42, 43, 44, 52, 54, 55, 56, 59, 64, 67, 68, 71, 75, 76, 79, 81. 85, 86, 87, 89 |
| Solve visual problems and patterns; complete a pattern to solve a problem | 2, 4, 6, 7, 13, 14, 19, 20, 23, 27, 29, 32, 35, 41, 42, 48, 50, 52, 53, 60, 61, 63, 65, 68, 69, 70, 72, 73, 76, 80, 82, 83, 84, 85, 86, 87, 88 |
| Graph ordered pairs or linear equations | 7, 65 |
| Estimate problem solutions | 8, 12, 14, 21, 67, 76 |
| Use logic to solve problems | 2, 6, 8, 10, 20, 21, 24, 32, 35, 36, 38, 46, 47, 69, 78, 83, 84 |
| Translate word problems into equations | 3, 9, 11, 13, 17, 26, 34, 38, 43, 55, 56, 64, 67, 68, 90 |
| Solve problems of probability, combinations, odds, permutations, random sampling, and statistics | 15, 22, 25, 28, 31, 33, 37, 44, 54, 55, 59, 67, 75, 81, 85, 86, 87, 89 |
| Use trial and error or mental math to solve problems | 2, 3, 6, 13, 16, 18, 23, 24, 39, 46, 64, 68, 69, 71, 72, 74, 77, 82, 85, 87 |
| Solve open-ended problems | 5, 22, 31, 39, 66 |
| Work backwards to solve problems | 16, 29, 30, 63, 90 |
| Solve multi-step problems | all conundrums |
| Choose an appropriate strategy to solve a problem | all conundrums |
| Use a variety of problem-solving strategies | all conundrums |
| Use quantitative reasoning | all conundrums |

# Grades 6-8 Common Core Standards
# Supported by the Conundrums

| Strand/Category | Standards |
|---|---|
| **Standards for Mathematical Practices** | • Make sense of problems and persevere in solving them<br>• Reason abstractly and quantitatively<br>• Construct viable arguments and critique the reasoning of others<br>• Model with mathematics<br>• Use appropriate tools strategically<br>• Attend to precision<br>• Look for and make use of structure<br>• Look for and express regularity in repeated reasoning |
| **The Number System** | • Apply and extend previous understandings of operations to add, subtract, multiply, and divide rational numbers<br>• Compute fluently with multi-digit numbers and find common factors and multiples<br>• Apply and extend previous understandings of numbers to the system of rational numbers |
| **Operations and Algebraic Thinking; Expressions and Equations** | • Apply and extend previous understandings of arithmetic to algebraic expressions; write and interpret numerical expressions<br>• Use properties of operations to generate equivalent expressions<br>• Reason about and solve one-variable equations and inequalities<br>• Represent and analyze quantitative relationships between dependent and independent variables<br>• Solve real-life and mathematical problems using numerical and algebraic expressions and equations<br>• Work with radicals and integer exponents<br>• Analyze and solve linear equations |
| **Measurement and Data** | • Convert like measurement units within a given measurement system<br>• Represent and interpret data<br>• Understand concepts of volume and relate volume to multiplication and to addition |
| **Geometry** | • Graph points on the coordinate plane to solve real-world and mathematical problems<br>• Solve real-world and mathematical problems involving angle measure, area, surface area, and volume (including the volume of cylinders, cones, and spheres)<br>• Draw, construct, and describe geometrical figures and describe the relationships between them<br>• Understand and apply the Pythagorean Theorem |
| **Ratio and Proportional Relationships** | • Understand ratio concepts and use ratio reasoning to solve problems<br>• Analyze proportional relationships and use them to solve real-world and mathematical problems |
| **Statistics and Probability** | • Develop understanding of statistical variability<br>• Summarize and describe distributions<br>• Use random sampling to draw inferences about a population<br>• Investigate chance processes and develop, use, and evaluate probability models |

# Thinking Skills Supported by the Conundrums

## Structure Based on Bloom's Taxonomy of Cognitive Development

| Cognitive Domain Levels *Simplest ⟶ Most Complex* | Skills | Conundrum Number(s) |
|---|---|---|
| **Remembering:** Recall data or information | arrange, define, describe, duplicate, label, list, match, name, order, recall, recognize, repeat, reproduce, select, state | Conundrums 1-90 |
| **Understanding:** Understand the meaning, translation, interpolation, and interpretation of instructions and problems. Explain concepts and state a problem in one's own words | classify, describe, discuss, explain, express, identify, indicate, locate, recognize, report, select, translate, paraphrase | Conundrums 1-90 |
| **Applying:** Use a concept in a new situation or unprompted use of an abstraction | apply, choose, demonstrate, dramatize, employ, illustrate, interpret, operate, practice, schedule, sketch, solve, use, write | Conundrums 1-90 |
| **Analyzing:** Distinguish among component parts to arrive at meaning or understanding | analyze, appraise, calculate, categorize, compare, contrast, criticize, differentiate, discriminate, distinguish, examine, experiment, question, test | Conundrums 1-90 |
| **Evaluating:** Justify a decision or position; make judgments about the value of an idea | appraise, argue, assess, defend, evaluate, judge, rate, select, support, value, compose, construct, create, design, develop, formulate, manage, organize, plan, set up, prepare, propose, write | Conundrums 1-90 |
| **Creating:** Create a new product or viewpoint | assemble, construct, create, design, develop, formulate, mold, prepare, propose, synthesize, write | Conundrums 6, 7, 8, 10, 12, 13, 14, 18, 19, 22, 23, 24, 26, 27, 31, 32, 34, 35, 38, 39, 50, 51, 52, 54, 60, 63, 66, 71, 72, 82, 85, 87 |

# Doing Math the Brain-Compatible Way

For a student to be skilled at math, he or she must be able to do far more than calculate, solve an equation, perform operations to find the answer to a word problem, or use a formula. Math is a language, requiring deep understandings of processes, relationships, abstract concepts, and nuances.

Brain-compatible learning theory is based on information that neuroscientists have learned about how the brain perceives, senses, processes, stores, and retrieves information. Brain-based learning principles offer useful strategies for doing math in ways that cement understanding, fix concepts and processes in long-term memory, and provide lifelong skills for applying math to many different situations and problems.

**Math understandings are deepened when a strategy, concept, problem, or process is . . .**

- connected to art, visuals, graphics, or color.

- presented with humor.

- related to real-life experiences and problems.

- presented in a setting in which you are invited to give feedback about it.

- connected to or learned in the context of a strong emotion.

- presented in a way that engages you personally.

- used in a variety of forms and manipulated in a variety of ways.

- applied to other situations with which you are already familiar.

- relevant to your interests and your life.

- used in situations where you are asked to explain (with writing, illustration, speaking, or otherwise) how you are thinking about it, how you have used it, and what it means.

- presented in a way that asks you to apply it to new or unexpected problems and situations.

- used settings where you discuss, share, explain, and demonstrate it with others.

- learned or applied in an environment that is relatively free from stress and threat.

# The
# 90
# Math Conundrums

# The Clever Scavenger

Rosco is a smart, scrappy rat who is always on the move. Like all rats, his major passion is food, and by necessity, he spends plenty of time seeking out tasty morsels. Rosco hustles around his city, locating all the places where spare morsels might be lying about. He's a frequent visitor to restaurant back doors, alleys with trash cans, and picnic sites. He knows the route of every garbage collector in the city, and all the hot dog vendors and cheese factory employees know him by name!

**Here are some statistics about Rosco's scavenging life:**

On January 1, 2011, Rosco celebrated his tenth birthday. On the morning of his second birthday, he began this daily schedule (for a 24-hour day):

- He has spent an average of just four hours a day sleeping.

- He has spent two and one-half times that long each day exploring the city with friends (always keeping his nose and eyes alert for possible future food-finding sites).

- He has spent the rest of the time scavenging and nibbling.

HOW MUCH TIME (UP TO HIS TENTH BIRTHDAY) HAD ROSCO SCAVENGED AND NIBBLED?

GIVE YOUR ANSWER IN HOURS.

Name_____

10

# The Pizza Mix-Up

It's a mystery!

Eight pizzas were delivered for Rosco Rat's party. Three of the pizzas were topped with cheese and sausage. The remaining five each had cheese and a different meat (not sausage). Unfortunately, every label fell off upon delivery and the meat on all the pizzas looked the same.

Alas! The mystery of which pizza was which could be solved only by tasting.

IT'S A DELICIOUS MYSTERY!

WHAT IS THE MINIMUM NUMBER OF TRIAL TASTES ROSCO COULD TAKE TO BE ABLE TO IDENTIFY EACH PIZZA?

Name_____

# A Matter of Age

During one of Rosco's birthday parties, four friends dropped in to celebrate. Quite remarkably, all of these friends shared the same birthday as Rosco although they were born in different years. The sum of their ages (at the time) was 24 years.

- Portia was one-third Meatball's age.

- Boomerang was three times Miles' age.

- Meatball was twice Boomerang's age.

- Two years later, Boomerang was twice Miles' age.

- Four years later, Portia was half Meatball's age.

WHAT WAS THE AGE DIFFERENCE BETWEEN THE YOUNGEST AND OLDEST OF THESE FOUR FRIENDS?

MEATBALL IS

MILES IS

PORTIA IS

BOOMERANG IS

Name_____

# Confusion on the Trail

At the end of a weary day, Rosco Rat comes to a spot where the paths diverge. Without a map, he's confused about which fork to take. All he knows for sure is that he wants the shortest route to a campground where he can rest for the night.

Arrange the numbers on each path to create the smallest whole number possible. Then, put a decimal point after the first digit on the left. This will show the lengths of the paths (in miles).

IF ROSCO IS LUCKY ENOUGH TO CHOOSE THE
SHORTEST PATH, WHERE WILL HE CAMP FOR THE NIGHT?

Name_____

# Money on His Mind

ONE CAN NEVER BE TOO RICH OR TOO FULL OF CHEESE.

Rosco Rat finds a bag of money on the sidewalk. To his amazement, the bag is filled with $10, $20, and $50 bills and it is labeled on the outside with the amount $8,800! Before he counts the money, he daydreams about how many combinations of bills could be inside.

If indeed there are only $10, $20, and $50 bills in the bag, and they do add up to $8,800 . . .

A . . . DESCRIBE AT LEAST FIVE DIFFERENT COMBINATIONS OF THE THREE KINDS OF BILLS THAT COULD BE IN THE BAG.

B . . . COULD THE NUMBER OF BILLS IN THE BAG BE 178?

(In the end, Rosco did the right thing. He turned the money over to the police and received a $100 reward for being a good citizen.)

Name_____

# A Tasty Endeavor

Rosco Rat is expecting his eight nieces and nephews for dinner. He wants to cut this olive and cheese pizza into eight slices with two olives on each slice.

It can be done using four, and only four, straight lines!
Cut the pizza for Rosco using only four straight lines.

### HINT:
THE SLICES DO NOT ALL
HAVE TO BE THE SAME
SIZE. AND REMEMBER,
THERE MUST BE TWO
OLIVES ON EACH SLICE!
*GOOD LUCK!*

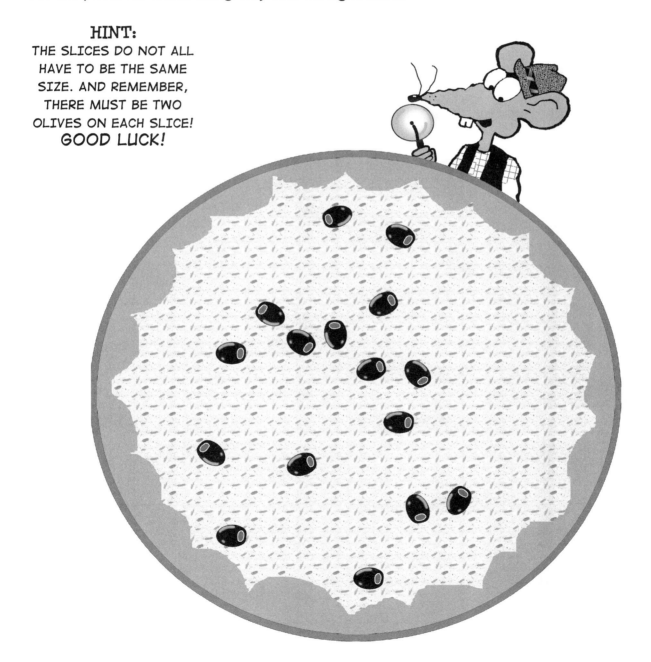

Name_____

# Favorite Finds

On any given day, Rosco sniffs out dozens of different edible morsels. It's amazing what food scraps litter the city. (How lucky for a hungry rat!)

The grid shows the location of a few of these delectable finds. When he gets to this section of the alley, Rosco follows a straight line to gobble up his favorite foods first. (Then he'll go back and wolf down the rest.) The line through his favorites is represented by this equation:

$$2x + 3 = y$$

PLOT THE LINE, AND COLOR ALL THE FOOD ITEMS THAT FALL ON THE LINE.

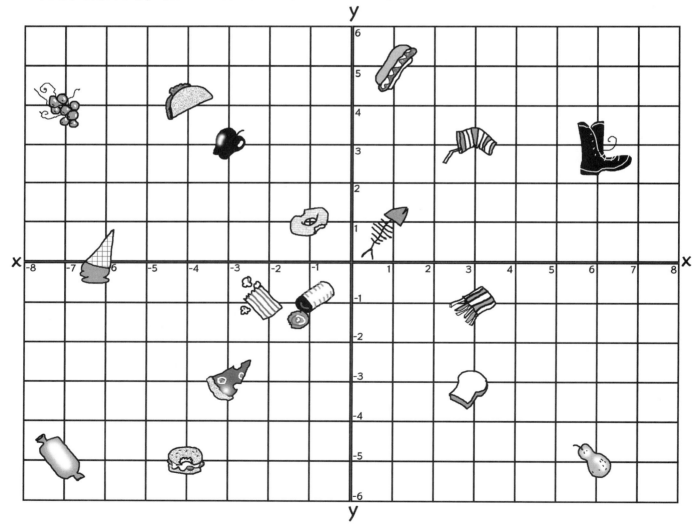

Name_____

16

# Filled to Capacity

A bakery in Rosco's neighborhood is having a fabulous sale on cream-filled, chocolate-covered pastries. Rosco wants to stock his refrigerator with as many of these scrumptious, ooey-gooey yummy bars as possible.

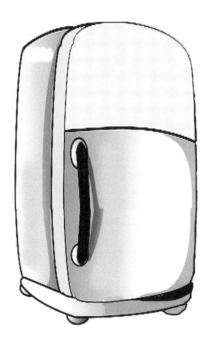

The measurement of a refrigerator is generally given in cubic feet capacity (how much interior space it has). This refrigerator is a 30-cubic-foot refrigerator. One-third is in the freezer. Inside, both compartments of the refrigerator measure 3 feet wide and 2.5 feet deep.

The pastry bars each measure 3 inches wide, 4 inches long, and 1 inch thick.

### ABOUT HOW MANY PASTRIES COULD BE IN THAT FREEZER? (CIRCLE ONE.)

| | | |
|---|---|---|
| 4500 | 1000 | 10,000 |
| 350    15,000 | 1600 | |
| 4300 | 1400 | 5000 |
| 6500 | 30,000 | 800 |

Name_____

# Bruised, Battered, and Broken

Rosco is a rodent of great athletic talent. However, when he pushes this talent to new heights, that tough body takes a beating.

While practicing new skateboard tricks (in particular, the 720° kickflip), he has had plenty of mishaps. In two weeks of practice (four hours a day every day), Rosco has sustained the following injuries:

14 bruises
28 cuts or scratches
2 sprained ankles
3 broken toes

Assume that Rosco can keep practicing, even with the impairments. If injuries and practices continue at this rate, which of the following will be greater?

- THE NUMBER OF BRUISES IN 11 DAYS OF PRACTICE

- THE NUMBER OF CUTS AND SCRATCHES IN 26 HOURS OF PRACTICE

- THE NUMBER OF BROKEN TOES IN 10 WEEKS OF PRACTICE

- THE NUMBER OF SPRAINED ANKLES IN 56 DAYS OF PRACTICE

Name_____

# Who's On Screech Street?

Rosco Rat and three friends are all set to go trick-or-treating. They'll each grab a different kind of candy container and head off in a different direction to knock on doors. Use the clues to figure out which one of the four will be trick-or-treating on Screech Street.

IN ORDER TO ANSWER THE QUESTION, YOU MIGHT WANT TO DRAW A TABLE OR CHART TO ORGANIZE THE CLUES!

*Meatball*   *Portia*   *Rosco*   *Boomerang*

## Clues:

The trick-or-treater who will carry a wicker basket is at one end of this line.

Boomerang will not be on Goblin Alley or Boo Boulevard.

Rosco will not carry the plastic jack-o-lantern container.

The trick-or-treater on Pumpkin Lane will not carry a pillowcase.

The Boo Boulevard trick-or-treater will carry a jack-o-lantern container.

Portia will not carry a plastic jack-o-lantern.

Portia is not next to the one who will be on Pumpkin Lane.

Boomerang will not carry a brown bag.

The friend who will collect candy in a brown bag is next to Rosco.

Rosco will not be on Goblin Alley.

WHO WILL BE TRICK-OR-TREATING ON SCREECH STREET? _____

Name_____

# Rescue at Sea

NEXT TIME – A BIGGER BOAT!

At sea, distances are measured in nautical miles. (A nautical mile is equal to 1.15 miles in the U.S. Customary system.) Speeds at sea are usually measured in knots. (A knot is one nautical mile per hour.)

Rosco Rat and Boomerang had traveled 231 nautical miles from Port Whiskers when they ran out of cheese and tuna fish. (Supposedly, they had enough food for the whole trip.) For Rosco, especially, this was a disaster! Thanks to a good cell phone, they were able to call for help.

The rescue boat—carrying plenty of cheese and tuna—left immediately from Port Whiskers. At exactly the same time, Rosco turned his boat around and headed back. The two boats traveled toward each other on the same route.

The boat carrying the food sailed at a speed of 21 knots.
Rosco and Boomerang sailed at a speed of 12 knots.

- FROM THE TIME THEY TURNED AROUND, HOW LONG DID ROSCO AND BOOMERANG HAVE TO WAIT FOR FOOD? (IN OTHER WORDS, HOW LONG WAS IT BEFORE THE TWO BOATS MET?)

- HOW FAR DID THE FOOD BOAT TRAVEL TO REACH ROSCO AND BOOMERANG?

Name_____

# Flying Spheres

The circumference of the baseball bouncing off Boomerang's head is nine inches.

The volume of the softball Rosco hopes to catch is about twenty-nine cubic inches.

WHICH IS THE BEST ESTIMATE OF THE DIFFERENCE BETWEEN THE RADIUS OF THE SOFTBALL AND THE RADIUS OF THE BASEBALL?

| | | |
|---|---|---|
| 3 in. | 1 in. | 1 in.$^2$ |
| 3.5 in. | 9 in.$^3$ | 2 in. |
| 0.5 in. | 3 in.$^2$ | 20 in.$^3$ |
| 1 in.$^3$ | 2 in.$^2$ | 0.5 in.$^2$ |

WRITE YOUR ANSWER INSIDE THE BASEBALL.

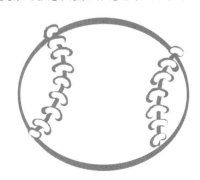

Name_____

# The Right Combination

### CASE FILE #13

Detective Rosco is hot on the trail of some stolen diamonds. The suspect is in custody, but Rosco needs to collect the evidence. He's learned the location where the diamonds are stashed; they're in a safe in an abandoned bakery.

All Rosco needs is to find the combination. He has a slip of paper showing all but one number. The suspect, Sneaky Pete Pilfer, won't tell the missing number. Pete believes he is smarter than any detective. In fact he's so confident no one will be able to get to the diamonds, that he gives clues about that missing number.

## CLUE 1:

15 - 22 - ___ - 5 - 38

## CLUE 2:

START WITH THREE CONSECUTIVE INTEGERS between -10 and 10. TWICE the THIRD is 13 greater than three TIMES the sum of the FIRST and the SECOND.

## CLUE 3:

If you ever FIND those INTEGERS (which you probably WON'T), MULTIPLY them together. Then DIVIDE by NEGATIVE two.

CAN YOU FIGURE OUT THE COMBINATION BEFORE DETECTIVE ROSCO DOES?

Name_____

22

# Celestial Geometry

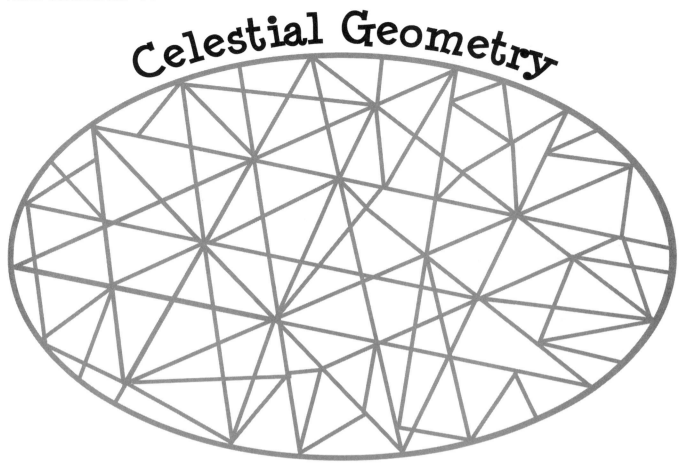

STARGAZE WITH ROSCO AT A KALEIDOSCOPE OF GEOMETRIC SHAPES.

See if you can find one (and only one) perfect five-sided star in the sky. Trace it with a marker or crayon and color it yellow.

WHICH OF THESE MEASUREMENTS IS THE BEST ESTIMATE OF THE STAR'S AREA?

$13 \text{ cm}^2$

$30 \text{ cm}^2$

$25 \text{ cm}^2$

$15 \text{ cm}^3$

$9 \text{ cm}^2$

USE CRAYONS OR MARKERS TO CREATE A KALEIDOSCOPE OF COLORS IN THE SKY.

Name_____

# The Daily Five

Boomerang Cat is sometimes found with a newspaper in his hands. Although he uses it most often in the litter box, he also reads it. Lately, he has been getting five newspapers a day.

STOCKS CONTINUE TO RISE TODAY ON THE BACK OF STRONG ECONOMIC DATA.

*Evening Chronicle*
Thursday, June 19
**Catastrophe at Local Pet Shop**

**The Sun Times**
*Thursday, June 19*
**Hero Cats Save Lives in Flood**

*The Daily Press*
Animal Rights Groups Protest Tainted Pet Food
*Thursday, June 19*

*Weekly Gazette* ——— *Week of June 15*
**Catherine Cattner Wins Mayoral Election**

**The Tidings**
*Thursday, June 19*
**$1,000,000 Reward**
**Offered for Missing Feline**

Today, he decides to read three of the five papers.

HOW MANY DIFFERENT COMBINATIONS OF THREE OF THESE PAPERS COULD HE READ?

_____

Assume that he changes his mind and reads all five papers.

HOW MANY DIFFERENT ARRANGEMENTS (PERMUTATIONS) ARE POSSIBLE FOR THE ORDER IN WHICH HE READS THE PAPERS?

_____

Name_____

24

# Time Matters

Portia Mouse's soccer team played an all-day tournament. Her team won the first two games, so they went on to the third game (the championship).

- Each game had two 30-minute halves plus a 15-minute break time.

- There was a one-hour break between games.

- Game One had two 3-minute timeouts for penalties and a 7-minute timeout for an injury.

- After the first 15 minutes of Game Two, a timeout was called for rain. This lasted 22 minutes.

- Game Three ended with a tie-breaking shoot-out that added 18 minutes to the total game time.

- After the third game, there was a 20-minute break before the Award Ceremony.

- The Award Ceremony lasted 30 minutes.

- Portia hung around with her teammates for another half-hour. She headed home at 3:58 PM.

**A.
WHAT TIME DID
GAME ONE BEGIN?**

**B.
WHAT TIME DID
GAME TWO RESUME
AFTER THE RAIN?**

Name_____

# Indigestion, Anyone?

Rosco Rat was born in the cellar of a cheese factory, so it's no wonder that anything cheesy is his favorite food.

He's been training for the State Cheese Dog Eating Championship, and his dog consumption increases every day.

At last count, Rosco ate 47 cheese dogs in ten minutes.
Two other competitors can eat an identical amount in 30 minutes.

HOW LONG WOULD IT TAKE ALL THREE TO POLISH OFF A PLATTER OF 47 CHEESE DOGS IF THEY ALL ATE THE DOGS TOGETHER?

I'M GETTING OUT OF HERE!

Name_____

26

# Painter's Problems

Rosco Rat is in a red mood today. This block is only one of the many things he has covered in red paint.

The block is a perfect cube with a total volume of **216 cubic inches.** He painted all sides of the cube red.

*IT LOOKS AS IF YOU CAUGHT ME RED-HANDED!*

WHAT WAS THE TOTAL SURFACE AREA PAINTED?

After the paint dried, Rosco decided to saw the block into one-inch cubes.

WHEN HE WAS FINISHED SAWING, HOW MANY OF THE CUBES WERE RED ON TWO (AND ONLY TWO) SIDES?

Name_____

# Tennis Troubles

Meatball is having some trouble with his tennis swing. He's hitting most of his strokes into the net.

Solve the puzzle in the net by finding the missing numbers. Note that the bottom row and the right-hand column have the same answer (the number in the lower right corner).

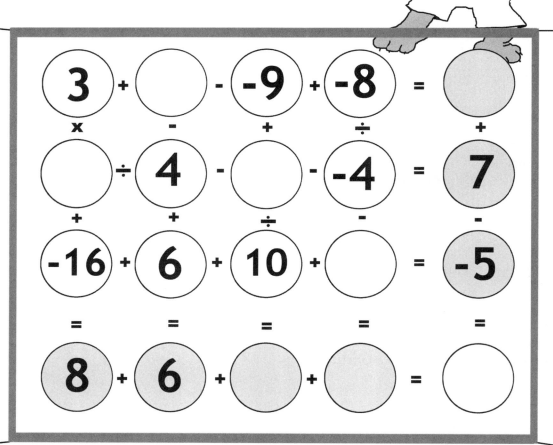

Name_____

# Who Won the Race?

It's too bad that Rosco overslept and missed the annual Cheddarville Rat Race run. Four of his nieces and nephews were participants. When he arrived, the little rats swarmed to greet him—all eager to report the results of the race. One (and only one) of the four did not tell the truth.

GOOD GOING, LITTLE DUDES!

"I FINISHED LAST, AGAIN."

"I CAME IN FIRST BY A MILE!"

"I DIDN'T FINISH FIRST OR LAST."

"AT LEAST I DIDN'T FINISH LAST."

LUCY    ARCHIE    CARLY    MILES

WHO WAS LYING?          WHO WON THE RACE?

_____          _____

Name_____

# Whisker Augmentation

On one of his scavenging trips, Rosco stumbled upon a half-used tube of an amazing potion.

He had always wanted more attention-getting whiskers. (Besides being attractive, his whiskers are great for feeling food in the dark!)

He tried the cream and waited hopefully for results.

- Assume that the miracle cream really did work well enough to double the number of whiskers and increase the length so that all the whiskers were triple the length of his originals.

- Assume that he started with four whiskers, each of which weighed .005 grams.

## WHAT IS THE WEIGHT OF ALL OF HIS WHISKERS NOW?

| | | |
|---|---|---|
| .12 g | .01 g | .05 g |
| .005 g | .5 g | .18 g |
| .002 g | .04 g | 2 g |
| 4 g | 5 g | 10 g |

Name_____

30

# Watch Out for the Spike!

The volley ball game is getting tense. The game is tied, and Meatball's team needs two points to win. Meatball—a notorious spiker—intends to smash that ball over the net into the floor. He has good reason to think he can: He's done this hundreds of times before.

WHACK!

The opposing team knows that Meatball is skilled at placing the spikes to the left, right, or center—wherever he chooses.

- OF MEATBALL'S LAST 120 SPIKES, 56 HAVE BEEN PLACED TO THE LEFT (ON THE OPPONENT'S SIDE OF THE NET).

- MEATBALL HAS SPIKED 34 OF THE LAST 72 SPIKES TO THE CENTER.

- OF THE LAST 210 SPIKES, HE HAS SENT THE BALL TO THE RIGHT 70 TIMES.

Assume you are the coach of the opposing team. Knowing the statistics about Meatball's spikes, where would you tell your players to expect his final spike to be directed?

EXPLAIN YOUR ANSWER.

Name_____

# Toothpick Puzzler

Rosco looks very thoughtful. He must be puzzling over the perplexing toothpick problem.

- Move just four toothpicks to make three squares.
  (Use real toothpicks or draw your result.)

- The squares must be the same size as the original four shown above.

- There should be no toothpicks left over.

Name_____

# Parachute Shortage

Too many students arrived for a discounted skydiving lesson. Instructors at the Fly & Dive Company were not prepared. They packed parachutes for only fifteen students, but thirty showed up.

The head instructor, Soren Dropp, decided on a fair (and clever) way to choose the students who could jump that day.

I DID IT!

## This is what he said he would do:

Everyone would get in a circle. He would start at one spot and count nine students (clockwise). The ninth student was to leave the circle. He would then count nine again (moving clockwise), starting with the student next to the one who had left. He would keep doing this until fifteen students were left.

Rosco wanted to be sure that he got a parachute. He also wanted his fourteen friends to be the others who were able to jump that day.

HOW SHOULD ROSCO ARRANGE HIMSELF AND HIS FRIENDS SO THAT ALL OF THEM WILL GET PARACHUTES?

*(Draw a diagram to show the arrangement.)*

Name_____

# Underwater Lunch

Boomerang swims in tropical waters for two reasons: it's good exercise, and if he's lucky, it's lunch!

## There are . . .

| | | |
|---|---|---|
| twelve **red** fish | three **blue** fish | six **striped** fish |
| nine **gold** fish | four **silver** fish | two **green** fish |

- If Boomerang actually catches a fish in his net, what is the probability that it will NOT be red? _____

- If he is lucky enough to catch two fish at once, what is the probability that they will both be green? _____

- Assume Boomerang catches two fish at once. Which of the following is likely to be the greatest?

    a. the probability that one will be striped and one will not be striped _____

    b. the probability that neither will be gold _____

    c. the probability that Boomerang will eat the fish without caring about the color _____

Name_____

# A Salty Solution

Rosco brought a live tuna back from his deep sea fishing trip. He planned to give the tuna to his friend Boomerang for his birthday and wanted to keep the fish in an environment as close to conditions in the ocean as possible. To solve this problem, he filled a wading pool with saltwater. To be precise, the water was a 30% saltwater solution. The pool, with a diameter of four feet, was filled to a depth of 12 inches.

The frisky fish splashed so much water out of the pool that the water depth changed to four inches.

Rosco filled the pool again to the original depth. The added water, which came straight from the hose, had no salt in it at all.

HE'LL LOVE IT!

Salt

WHAT WAS THE STRENGTH OF THE SALTWATER SOLUTION AFTER ROSCO FILLED THE POOL THE SECOND TIME?

EXPLAIN HOW YOU ARRIVED AT YOUR CONCLUSION ABOUT THE SOLUTION.

Name_____

# It Must Be Magic!

Rosco's assistant, Portia Mouse, refuses to be sawed in half!

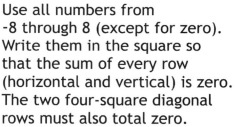

Rosco the Magician turns to less risky (but still mysterious) tricks: pulling rabbits from hats and making magic with math. Here is one of Rosco's magic math squares.

SEE HOW FAST YOU CAN FILL IT IN.

Use all numbers from -8 through 8 (except for zero). Write them in the square so that the sum of every row (horizontal and vertical) is zero. The two four-square diagonal rows must also total zero.

Name_____

# Up With Raisins!

Portia Mouse found a bag of stale oatmeal and raisin cookies. She hates oatmeal, and loves raisins. She decided to pick out the raisins and make a pie!

Portia collected two and one-fourth cups of raisins from the cookies for her pie. Each full cup held 96 raisins. Each cookie contained an average of nine raisins.

HOW MANY COOKIES DID PORTIA USE?

TWO AND A QUARTER CUPS OF GOODNESS!

Name_____

# Sloppy Eating

Rosco did his homework. That's the good news. The bad news is that he couldn't resist eating while he worked. The paper is splattered with drips of mustard from his cheese dog. Some of his good work is impossible to read!

OOOPS!

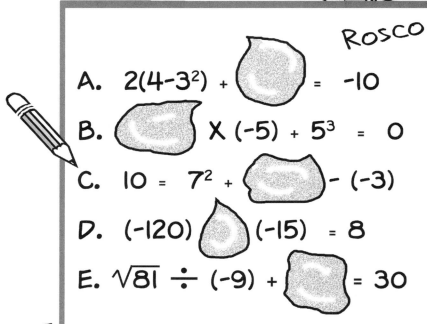

Rosco

A. $2(4-3^2) +$ ⬤ $= -10$

B. ⬤ $\times (-5) + 5^3 = 0$

C. $10 = 7^2 +$ ⬤ $- (-3)$

D. $(-120)$ ⬤ $(-15) = 8$

E. $\sqrt{81} \div (-9) +$ ⬤ $= 30$

I KNOW I ACED IT, TOO!

Assume that all his answers are correct. Figure out what number and/or symbol is missing from each equation on the paper.

Name_____

38

# What's the Problem?

Here's the solution to a problem for Rosco:

## 13

But what's the problem? You figure it out!

Circle the number of any problem that matches the solution. (There might be more than one!)

**1** It is 3:30 PM. Rosco has been on the beach since 8:45 AM. On the average, he's eaten a cheese snack every half hour. What's the number of snacks Rosco has eaten?

**2** A sand castle on the beach is 3.25 feet wide, 4 feet long, and 2.5 feet tall. How many square feet of the beach does the sand castle cover?

**3** The summer season is almost over. Rosco has worked 54 days at the beach canteen, and has 3 more days to go. So far, he has drunk 270 liters of grape soda. At this rate, how many liters will he drink?

**4** The distance to the water from Rosco's beach blanket is 30 feet. He goes into the ocean about 39 times a day. If he eats a hot dog for every 180 feet he runs, how many hot dogs must he purchase each day?

**5** Rosco jumped into his boat and rowed toward his sinking friend, Boomerang, 650 feet away. His boat moved at 40 feet per minute. Boomerang swam toward Rosco at 10 feet per minute. How many minutes did it take Rosco to reach him?

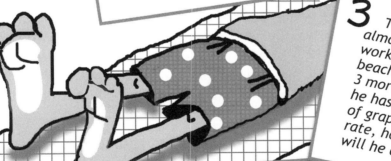

Name_____

# Football Fanatics

Rosco Rat and his friends are great football fans, in any kind of weather!

Review the rules about scoring in the game of football. Use that information to solve some football scoring questions.

There are four ways to score in the game of football. Only the team in possession of the ball can score (except for a safety).

| Touchdown | 6 points | The ball must be carried or caught in the end zone. |
|---|---|---|
| Extra Point(s) | 1 or 2 points | After a touchdown, get 1 extra point by kicking the ball through the goal posts or 2 extra points by running or passing the ball over the goal line. |
| Field Goal | 3 points | Kick the ball from the field through the goal posts. |
| Safety | 2 points | The opposing team gets 2 points if the player carrying the ball is tackled behind his own goal line. |

A sports reporter announced these final scores for Friday Night Football. Which of them is not possible?

19 to 4      27 to 0

8 to 1      44 to 6

The final score of the game was:

**Home Team   30      Visitors   25**

Describe two different ways the teams could have arrived at these scores.

Name_____

# Coin Confusion

Rosco is puzzling over a confusing coin problem he found in a puzzle book. He'd like to solve the puzzle himself, but he needs some help.

**Can you solve this common "cents" dilemma? Here are the instructions:**

- Pick eight coins that equal fifty cents.

- The coins that remain must also equal fifty cents.

- When you've taken them, the coins that remain must form a pattern of squares identical in shape to the pattern of the empty squares.

## WHICH COINS SHOULD ROSCO TAKE?

Untangle the confusion by drawing a line to separate the coins into two groups according to the instructions.

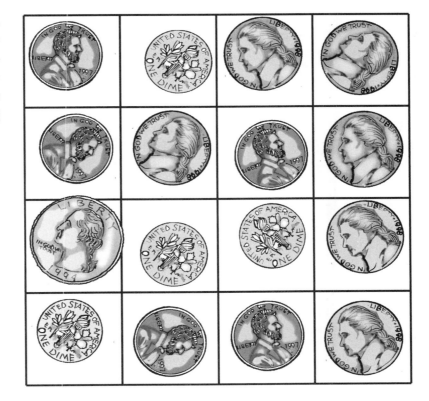

Name

Math Conundrums—Learning Adventures Series

| Surface Gravity | |
| --- | --- |
| Mercury | 0.38 |
| Venus | 0.9 |
| Earth | 1 |
| Mars | 0.38 |
| Jupiter | 2.7 |
| Saturn | 1.2 |
| Uranus | 0.93 |
| Neptune | 1.5 |

# Lost in Space

Surface gravity is not the same on all planets in space. The chart shows the surface gravity (in relation to Earth) for the eight planets in our solar system. This means that beings have different weights on different planets.

Assume that 18-pound Boomerang lands on a distant planet and encounters a 4-ounce blowfish there. Assume also that on this planet Boomerang weighs 6.84 pounds and the blowfish weighs .095 pounds.

ON WHICH PLANET HAVE THEY LANDED?

Name_____

42

# A Diving Dilemma

Rosco is a descendent of river rats.
He loves the water.

Notice that he dives and enters the water at an angle. Once he hits the water, Rosco continues descending at the same angle for ten feet, until he hits the bottom.

Then he pushes up off the bottom and shoots straight up to the surface.
This distance is eight feet.

When Rosco entered the water, he was seven feet from the end of the dock.

*HOW FAR AWAY FROM THE DOCK WAS HE WHEN HE CAME TO THE SURFACE?*

You might want to draw
a diagram to help with
the solution to this dilemma.

Name_____

# Take a Break!

Today is not a smooth day for Rosco and his friends. Many of them need to take a break from each other.

- Boomerang is tired of Rosco's bragging and Portia's complaining.

- Rosco is downright sick of Meatball hanging around and being so bossy.

- Poor Carly can't get a wink of sleep, due to Boomerang's snoring.

- Lucy is too shy to hang around with anyone except her brother Miles.

- Portia Mouse finds Rosco's tall tales amusing, but not his giant ego.

- Neither Carly nor Miles is afraid of spiders, but they're both allergic to cats.

- Meatball is fed up with Portia's bad temper and Carly's whines.

Give the characters a break! Figure out which pairs CAN be together. Then follow grid lines to draw walls, making private "forts" that include two characters. Each of the "forts" must be identical in size and shape.

Don't put any pairs together that will annoy each other!

C - Carly
M - Miles
P - Portia
B - Boomerang
R - Rosco
Mb - Meatball
L - Lucy

Name_____

# The Race Isn't Over

Rosco is running hard in this race. (That just may be because fried cheese sticks are being served at the Finish Line!) In this picture, we can't see the other seven competitors, so we don't know how he's doing at this point in the race. Use the following clues to find out.

### CLUES

- Five runners are behind #22.
- #16 is two runners ahead of #22.
- Runner #9 is ahead of #4 but is three runners behind Rosco.
- There are three runners between Rosco and #4.
- #7 is three runners ahead of #11.
- #13 is just behind #11.

A. WHAT IS ROSCO'S CURRENT PLACE IN THIS RACE?

B. IF #13 WINS THE RACE, HOW MANY RUNNERS WILL HE OR SHE HAVE TO PASS?

Name_____

# Pizza Probabilities

Rosco brought seven pizzas home for a quiet night of pizza and TV.

Each one is sliced into eight equal slices. In addition to cheese, these are the toppings:

| | |
|---|---|
| Pizza 1 | sausage and salami |
| Pizza 2 | salami and mushrooms |
| Pizza 3 | bacon, olives, and mushrooms |
| Pizza 4 | onions and green peppers |
| Pizza 5 | sausage and mushrooms |
| Pizza 6 | half pepperoni, half sausage |
| Pizza 7 | pepperoni and sausage |

Rosco reaches into a box and takes a slice (without looking).

A. WHAT IS THE PROBABILITY THAT THE SLICE WILL HAVE SAUSAGE ON IT?

B. WHAT IS THE PROBABILITY THAT IT WILL NOT HAVE MUSHROOMS?

C. WHAT IS THE PROBABILITY THAT IT WILL HAVE NEITHER BACON NOR ONION?

Assume that, instead of grabbing one slice, Rosco grabs two (from two different boxes).

D. WHAT IS THE PROBABILITY THAT ONE WILL HAVE PEPPERONI AND ONE WILL HAVE BACON?

Name_____

46

# Hang Ten?

When a surfer "hangs ten," he or she has feet placed on a surfboard so that all ten toes hang over the edge. "Hang five" is the term used when just one foot is positioned so that all the toes hang over.

On this particularly fine surfing day, Rosco is practicing in the big waves with several other surfers. (They are all humans with ten toes each.)

- One-fourth of the other surfers are hanging five.

- Three-eighths of the other surfers are hanging NO toes over any surfboard edges.

- The rest of the other surfers, not counting Rosco, are hanging ten.

- There are a total of 120 toes hanging in this competition.

A. HOW MANY SURFERS ARE PRACTICING TODAY (INCLUDING ROSCO)?

B. HOW MANY SURFERS ARE HANGING TEN?

WHAT STRATEGY DID YOU USE TO SOLVE THIS PROBLEM?

Name_____

# Many Right Answers

Ms. Portia asked her students to think of a number with the following characteristics:

- a five-digit odd number
- middle digit is the largest
- middle digit is odd
- all digits are different
- 8 is not one of the digits
- digit in hundreds place is odd
- digit in ten thousands place < 5
- the sum of the digits is 17

These smart little rat students followed the teacher's directions precisely.
None of the rats came up with the same numbers. And ALL the rats had right answers!

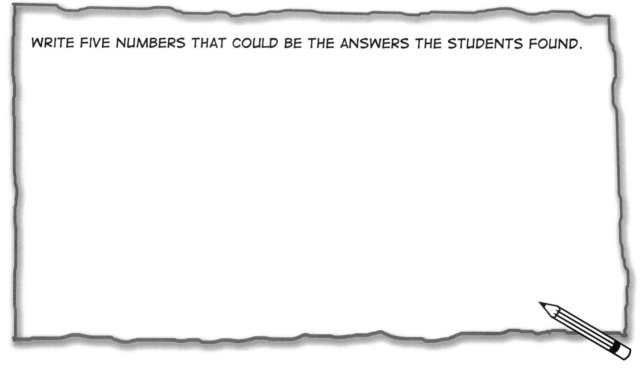

WRITE FIVE NUMBERS THAT COULD BE THE ANSWERS THE STUDENTS FOUND.

Name_____

# Milkshake Metrics

In December of 2007, Taka and Toshi of Japan set a world record for the fastest time to drink a 500-milliliter milkshake through a straw. This amazing and tasty feat was completed in nine seconds.

*I DON'T LIKE TO BOAST, BUT I WAS THAT FAST AT ICE CREAM INHALING WHEN I WAS A PUP!*

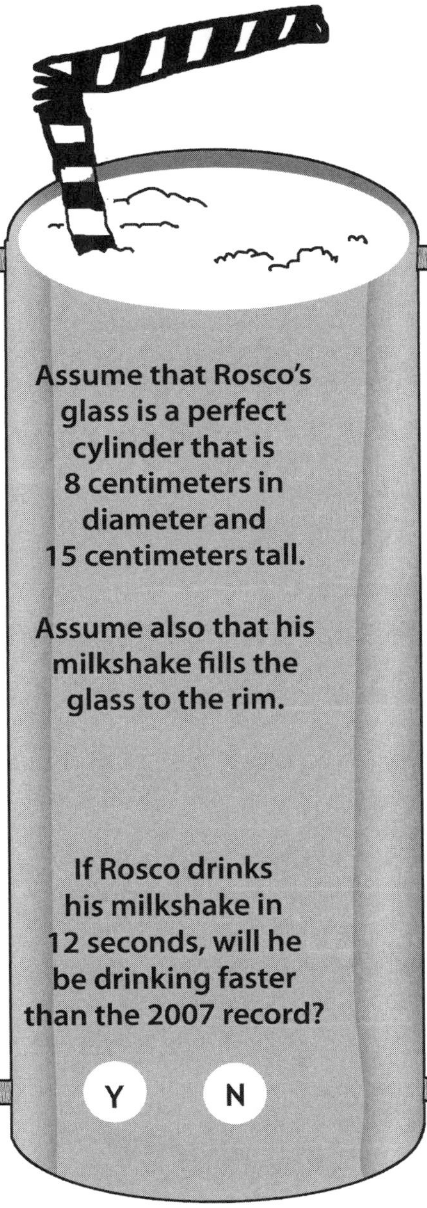

**Assume that Rosco's glass is a perfect cylinder that is 8 centimeters in diameter and 15 centimeters tall.**

**Assume also that his milkshake fills the glass to the rim.**

**If Rosco drinks his milkshake in 12 seconds, will he be drinking faster than the 2007 record?**

Y    N

SHOW THE WORK YOU DID TO ARRIVE AT YOUR SOLUTION.

*Note: To solve this problem, you will have to explore the relationship between milliliters and cubic centimeters.*

Name_____

# Honeycomb Puzzler

Boomerang would like to solve this honeycomb puzzle to show Ms. Portia Mouse that he is smarter than he looks. But the sweet smell of the flowers and the drone of the honey bees make him drowsy. Help Boomerang solve this puzzle before he drops off to sleep.

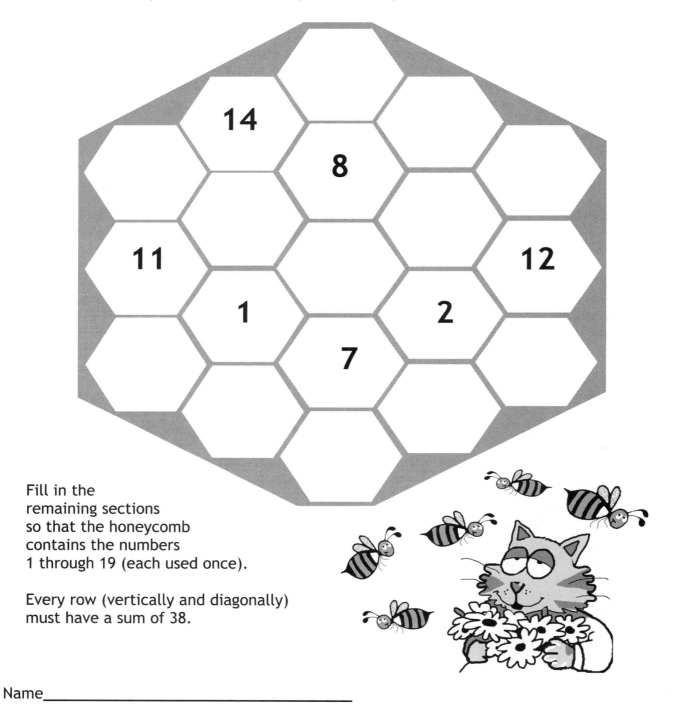

Fill in the remaining sections so that the honeycomb contains the numbers 1 through 19 (each used once).

Every row (vertically and diagonally) must have a sum of 38.

Name_____

# Strange Laws

There are some very unusual laws for cats. Solve this conundrum to find out about three of them.

To crack the code below, you will need to solve 14 problems and translate the answers into letters for the missing words.

GUILTY AS CHARGED!

Today: **Cat Cases**
Judge Portia
Presiding

SOLVE EACH EQUATION TO FIND THE VALUE OF X.

1. $4x - 7 = -11$
2. $-x + 9 = -3$
3. $100 - x^2 = 19$
4. $20 - 27 = -x$
5. $(x \div 4) + 7 = 9$
6. $5(x + 6) = 130$
7. $x^2 - 50 = -25$
8. $x^2 = 16$
9. $(123 \div x) = 41$
10. $-4(3 + 6) = 2x$
11. $3x = 69$
12. $x^5 = 32$
13. $4x = 12 + 3x$
14. $-40 + x = -21$

Each number answer stands for the letter with that position in the alphabet. (It doesn't matter if the answer is positive or negative.) For instance, if x = 4 or –4, write D in the blanks above that problem number.

**A. In Zion, IL, it is illegal for anyone to give this to a cat:**

___ ___ ___ ___ ___ ___ ___ ___   ___ ___ ___ ___ ___
1   2   3   4   5   6   7   8    9   3   4   1   10

**B. In Sterling, CO, a cat cannot (legally) run loose without wearing:**

___ ___ ___ ___ ___   ___ ___ ___ ___ ___
1   6   1   3   2    2   3   4   5   6

**C. In Cresskill, NJ, cats must do this to warn birds they are nearby:**

___ ___ ___ ___   ___ ___ ___ ___ ___   ___ ___ ___ ___ ___
11  7   1   10   6   5   10  7   7    12  7   13  2   14

Name_____

# An Exercise in Excess

Rosco ordered samples from the world's greatest cheesemakers. He intended to eat them all in one week. But so many samples arrived, that he's not sure if he can!

**MONDAY**

Rosco ate $\frac{1}{5}$ of the total number.

**TUESDAY**

Rosco ate $\frac{1}{6}$ of the original number.

**WEDNESDAY**

Rosco ate $\frac{2}{9}$ of the original number.

**THURSDAY**

Rosco ate half as many as he ate on Wednesday.

**FRIDAY**

Rosco was so bloated that he only ate two small samples.

At the end of the week, there were 160 samples left.

HOW MANY CHEESE SAMPLES WERE ORIGINALLY DELIVERED TO ROSCO?

Name_____

# Missing Out

When Meatball the Bulldog is one of the drivers, the Speed Cup Race is always sold out. (Obviously, he has many faithful fans.) A total of 14,400 tickets were gone long before race day.

- At the start of the race, 75% of the ticket holders had entered the gates and taken their seats.

- Another 21% of the ticket holders came late.

- Of the total fans who came to the race, 25% left early.

- It's too bad that many of Meatball's fans missed the fantastic (surprise) finish. He came from far behind to win the race.

- Of the 14,400 fans who bought tickets, how many missed seeing Meatball cross the finish line?

Name_____

# Mac & Cheese To Go

WELL, GRANDSON, I'VE GOT TMJ,
AND SHINGLES, AND CATARACTS,
AND BILIOUSNESS, AND ARTHRITIS,
AND BUNIONS, AND

POOR GRANNY!

Rosco Rat is going to visit his sick grandmother in the country.

Because she's too ill to make her famous macaroni and cheese casserole, Rosco decides that he must take some on his trip. So he prepares several pans and puts them in his freezer.

When Rosco gets ready to pack, he has the job of fitting the macaroni and cheese pans into his suitcase.

Rosco's suitcase measures 16 inches long, 12 inches wide and 6 inches deep.

Each pan of macaroni and cheese is 7 inches long, 5 inches wide, and 2.5 inches deep.

**HOW MANY PANS OF MAC AND CHEESE CAN HE FIT INTO HIS SUITCASE?**

Rosco wonders whether he'll get more volume if he lines the inside of the suitcase with plastic and fills it with macaroni and cheese out of the pans. He'll have to thaw the food, of course, so that every possible space in the suitcase is packed full.

**IF HE CHOOSES THIS METHOD OF PACKING, HOW MANY PANS OF MACARONI AND CHEESE WILL HE NEED TO THAW AND USE?**

Name_____

# Key Question

As the new security guard for an apartment building, Meatball has a key to every one of the twelve apartments. During his first week on the job, all the tenants went on vacation. Meatball agreed to visit each tenant's apartment daily to water their plants.

Disaster struck! All the labels fell off his master set of keys, and he doesn't have a clue which key will open which door. Meatball could lose his job if he doesn't get this dilemma resolved.

WHAT IS THE MAXIMUM NUMBER OF TRIES MEATBALL WILL HAVE TO TAKE TO GET ALL THE KEYS LABELED CORRECTLY?

Write your answer on the key.

Name_____

# Against the Flow

The river flows at an average of 12 mph.

Rosco's average paddling rate is 28 mph.

This mighty kayaker is not afraid of any challenge on the river. On this trip, he has chosen to paddle against the flow of the river for the length of the 240-mile river. When he finishes this trip, he will turn around and paddle back the other way!

A. HOW LONG DOES THE FIRST HALF OF THE TRIP TAKE ROSCO RAT?

B. HOW DOES THE TIME OF THE RETURN TRIP DIFFER FROM THE FIRST HALF—PADDLING AT THE SAME RATE WITH THE RIVER INSTEAD OF AGAINST IT?

Name_____

# Golf Trivia

The answers to these golf trivia questions can be formed by pulling digits from the golf balls that Rosco has hit at the driving range.

FIND THE NUMBERS IN THE ORDER THAT THE PROBLEMS ARE GIVEN. USE EACH DIGIT ONLY ONE TIME. CROSS OUT DIGITS AS YOU USE THEM.

1. number (in thousands) of golf courses in the U.S. *(2-digit even number; sum of digits is 7; product is 6)*

2. last year that golf balls stuffed with feathers were used *(4-digit number; 3 digits even; hundreds and ones digits are the same; sum of digits is 21; product is 256)*

3. number (in millions) of people who play golf each year in the U.S. *(prime number < 10 and > 3)*

4. average distance (in meters) from the tee to the hole on a miniature golf course *(the smallest 2-digit number possible with remaining digits)*

5. age of youngest golfer to shoot a hole in one *(single odd digit > 4)*

6. number of dimples on a regulation golf ball *(smallest number possible using all the remaining digits)*

Name_____

# Music Makes "Cents"

The Rappin' Rebels Band released a new CD, *Back Alley Blues*.
The album will sell for $14.00.

Fourteen percent of the retail price of the CD is guaranteed for royalties to the producer, the writers, and the performers.

For the purpose of royalties, each song is treated equally. (The retail value of each song would be $2.00, since there are seven songs.)

On each song, the 14% royalty is split this way:
   2% to the producer
   6% to the songwriter
   6% to the performer

If there is more than one writer or performer, the amount is split evenly among them.
Rosco is the producer of all the songs.

| Song | Writer(s) | Performer(s) |
|---|---|---|
| 1 Back Alley Blues | Rosco & B.B.Catman | Rosco Rap |
| 2 Cat's Claw | B.B. Catman | The Rappin' Rebels |
| 3 Rat Race | Rosco Rap | Portia Petty |
| 4 Leave Me Alone | Portia Petty | The Rappin' Rebels |
| 5 Munster Heaven | Rosco Rap | Rosco Rap |
| 6 Tuna Blues | Rosco & B.B.Catman | The Rappin' Rebels |
| 7 On the Run | Rosco Rap & Portia Petty | The Rappin' Rebels |

**HOW MANY CDs WILL HAVE TO SELL BEFORE ROSCO MAKES $1000?**

Name_____

58

# The One That Gets Away

Usually Boomerang is an expert at catching fish.
But this particular fish keeps getting away.
Just when it's seemingly headed right for the
hook, it turns and heads the other way.

Use real toothpicks and a button (or penny)
to create the fish shown below.

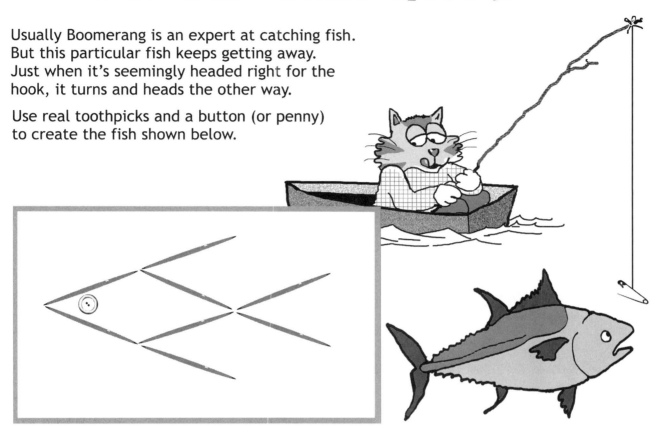

Move the button and just three toothpicks to make the fish swim the opposite direction.
**DRAW YOUR SOLUTION HERE.**

Name_____

# Too Much, Too Little

Whew! What a workout! Rosco Rat spent a long time
at the gym today using a total of five different machines.

- On the shoulder press, he set the weight at 8 pounds. He did 3 sets of 20 presses. Each set took 2.5 minutes.

- He did 4 sets of 15 leg lifts. Each time he lifted 10 pounds. Each set took 1 minute.

- On the abdominal machine, he moved 15 pounds with each repetition. He did 2 sets of 30 repetitions. Each set took 4 minutes.

- He visited the soda machine 3 times, taking 4 minutes each time to drink an 8-ounce soda.

- The last stop was the treadmill where he ran at a rate of 6 miles per hour.

## HOW LONG DID ROSCO SPEND ON THE TREADMILL?

**There are two problems with the problem above!
There is information that is NOT needed to solve the
problem and some necessary information is missing.**

A. Circle any information that is not needed to solve the problem.

B. Describe the information that is missing, but needed to solve the problem.

_____

_____

_____

Name_____

# Where Did He Go Wrong?

$$5x - 9 = 3x + 15$$

$$5x - 9 + 9 = 3x + 15 - 9$$

$$5x = 3x + 6$$

$$5x - 3x = 3x + 6 - 3x$$

$$\frac{2x}{2} = \frac{6}{2}$$

$$2x = 6$$

The homework didn't get Boomerang's full attention tonight. As a result, he has not solved this problem correctly.

EXAMINE BOOMERANG'S WORK.

CIRCLE THE STEP IN THE EQUATION WHERE BOOMERANG WENT WRONG.

FIX THE PROBLEM TO FIND THE CORRECT SOLUTION.

Name_____

# Follow Your Nose

Rosco Rat knows cheese pizza when he smells it. So he follows a trail of prime numbers to a secret back entrance to the kitchen. Mark Rosco's trail with your pencil.

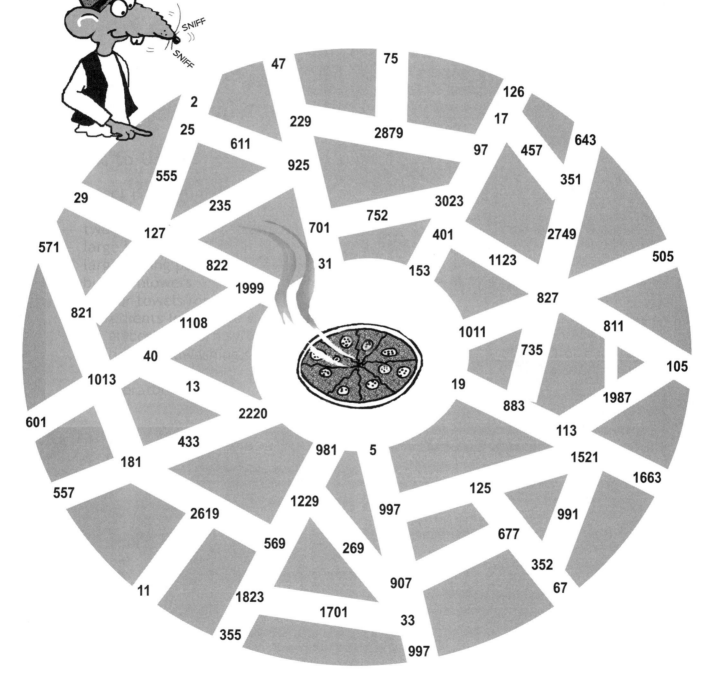

THAT WAY! THE NOSE KNOWS!

SNIFF

SNIFF

Name_____

62

# Handshakes All Around

The relay race is intense, and Rosco and his friends are fierce competitors. But when the race is over, the players shake hands all around and congratulate each other.

Each relay team has six players. Each of the twelve racers shakes hands with every other racer one time.

**HOW MANY HANDSHAKES WILL THERE BE?**

Use this space to figure out the number of handshakes.

Name_____

# Laundry Quandry

The most common quandary in the laundry is the disappearance of socks. Curiously, it is usually just one sock in a pair that disappears. Every time she does the laundry, Portia Mouse ends up with fewer pairs of socks!

Portia learns that socks have been disappearing at the Tidy Suds Laundromat since it opened five years ago.

Of the last **2673** pairs of socks that were washed and dried in the machines here, **891** individual socks were never seen again. Every lost sock was ONE of a PAIR!

TODAY, PORTIA IS WASHING NINE PAIRS OF SOCKS. IF THE RATE OF DISAPPEARANCE HOLDS, HOW MANY SOCKS CAN SHE EXPECT TO TAKE HOME?

I FIGURE IT'S EITHER THE SOCK MONSTER, OR A ONE-LEGGED BANDIT!

Name_____

64

# Bring on the Tuna

Boomerang prefers tuna above all other flavors. When he eats dry cat food, he hopes it has some tuna flavor mixed in.

THERE SHOULD BE NO SKIMPING ON THE TUNA!

BRAND X

Brand Y

Today he is about to sample two different brands of dry cat food. The first dish contains six cups of a mixture that is 20% tuna. The second dish contains four cups of a mixture that is 60% tuna. He is eager to put these products to a taste test!

He sniffs the first dish and knows right away there is not enough fish for his taste. The second dish smells more promising. He decides to mix the contents of the two dishes to increase the intensity of the fish flavor for his entire snack.

WHAT IS THE PERCENTAGE OF TUNA FLAVOR IN BOOMERANG'S FINAL MIXTURE?

Name_____

# Picking Up Speed

Rosco Rat is a big fan of winter sports.

Today, he and Boomerang are sledding down a hill that has a consistent slope.

They start at a speed of 3 miles per hour. With each 20 feet traveled, the speed increases by 10% over the original speed.

HOW MANY FEET WILL THE SLED TRAVEL BEFORE ITS SPEED EXCEEDS 5 MPH?

_____

IF THE SLEDDING HILL IS 160 FEET LONG, HOW FAST WILL THE SLED BE TRAVELING AT THE END?

_____

Name_____

# On the Edge

Mrs. Webster, a nosy neighbor of Rosco Rat, is intrigued by a mysterious package that has arrived for him.

She crawls along *every* edge (and this includes the bottom edges) looking for a way to peek inside. Unfortunately, the spider is unable to satisfy her curiosity. She'll have to wait until Rosco comes home!

The box measures
50 centimeters long,
30 centimeters wide,
and 35 centimeters tall.

I JUST *HAVE* TO KNOW WHAT'S INSIDE!

Rosco Rat
Garbage Can #12
Backstreet Alley
USA

WHAT IS THE LONGEST DISTANCE THE SPIDER CAN CRAWL
(STAYING *ONLY* ON THE EDGES) WITHOUT RE-TRACING ANY OF HER STEPS?

Name_____

# Good News

Boomerang is a news fan. He's particularly fond of animal stories and the classified ads about cats for adoption. His attraction to newspapers began because he found that crumpled newspapers are good for making cozy sleeping nooks in cold alleys, good for shredding up to make kitty litter, and good for rolling up to use as fly swatters.

Since he was a small kitty back in the beginning of 2006, Boomerang has been reading and collecting newspapers three times a week.

HOW MANY NEWSPAPERS HAS HE READ SINCE THE FIRST WEEK OF JANUARY, 2006?

Name_____

# Puzzling Over Pascal

Way back in 1655, a French mathematician named Blaise Pascal published this arrangement of numbers in a triangle. The numbers form an interesting pattern of special relationships between the numbers. It has come to be known as "Pascal's Triangle."

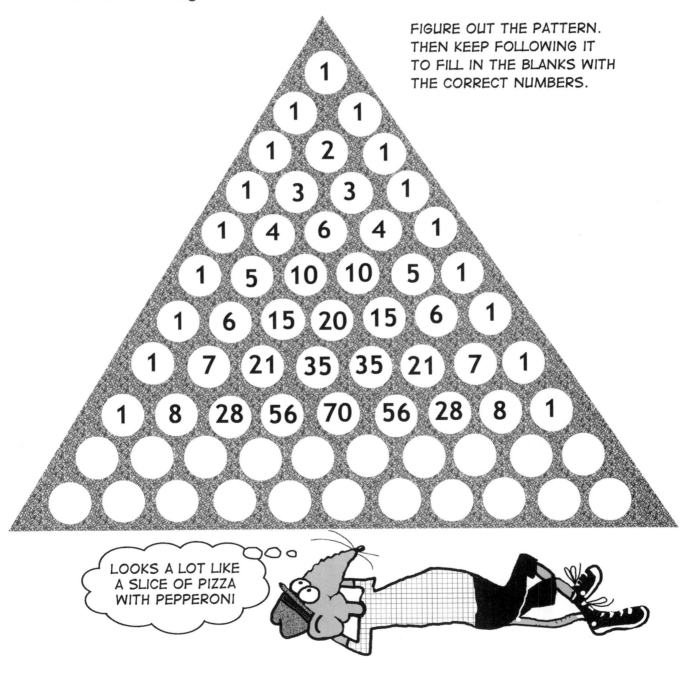

FIGURE OUT THE PATTERN. THEN KEEP FOLLOWING IT TO FILL IN THE BLANKS WITH THE CORRECT NUMBERS.

LOOKS A LOT LIKE A SLICE OF PIZZA WITH PEPPERONI

Name_____

# To Swat or Not to Swat?

Rosco Rat is constantly bothered by flies and other crawling or flying creatures.

HE SWATS THESE FLIES.

HE CHOOSES NOT TO SWAT THESE FLIES.

GIVEN THE ATTRIBUTES OF THE FLIES HE SWATS AND LEAVES ALONE, WHICH OF THESE WILL HE PROBABLY LEAVE ALONE?

Name_____

# Edible Geometry

Portia's Pastry Palace makes giant oatmeal-raisin cookies in two super sizes.
Rosco and Boomerang have ordered one cookie each in different shapes.
Both cookies are one inch thick.

Rosco's round cookie has a 16-inch diameter. Not too surprisingly, he ate only $\frac{7}{8}$ of it.

The cookie Boomerang ate is a 14-inch square. He ate only $\frac{5}{6}$ of it!

WHICH FRIEND ATE MORE COOKIE (IN TOTAL VOLUME)?

Name_____

# Headed for Trouble!

It looks as if Rosco is headed for trouble.
You can help him navigate Bone-breaker Boulevard.
Solve this long, winding problem correctly, and he
just might avoid a major crash along the way.
Read ALL the directions below before you start.

$\sqrt{121}$  $6^2$  9.09  $-50.91$  100  $35\% \cdot 40$  $7^2$  $(-70)$  $\frac{2}{5} \cdot 120$  $\sqrt{169}$  $5(2^3)$  56  $-4 \cdot 6$  85.15  $\frac{3}{25} \cdot \frac{5}{4}$  $60\% \cdot 45$  $-\sqrt{10,000}$  $2^6$  $\sqrt[3]{125}$  $= 30$

GRRR!

As Rosco moves along the sidewalk, he must ADD
the value of each section to the previous section.
However, when he comes to one of the seven sections
with obstructions, he must leap over it and SUBTRACT
the value of that section. When he gets to the end,
he will have a total of 30.

FIND THE CORRECT NUMBER FOR THE BLANK SECTION.

Name_____

# Cheeses of All Ages

MINE, ALL MINE!

Rosco is taking stock of his aged, imported cheese supply.
Here are some clues to help you find out just how young or old these cheeses are.

- ✓ Thirty-nine is the sum of the ages of all eight cheeses on the table.
- ✓ Three of the cheeses are the same age, one year younger than any of the others.
- ✓ Four of the other cheeses are one year apart in age.
- ✓ The remaining cheese is **twenty-two time**s the age of the youngest cheese!

**WHICH EQUATION WILL HELP YOU FIND THE AGE OF THE YOUNGEST CHEESE?**

a) $22 = 39 - 4x - 3x$

b) $3x + (x + 1) + (x + 2) + (x + 3) + (x + 4) + 22x = 39$

c) $3x + 4x + 4 + 22x = 39$

d) $7x + 22x = 39$

Use the equation to find the age of the youngest cheese.

_____

Then find the age of the oldest cheese.

_____

Name_____

# Mail on the Move

Just as Meatball, the mailman, reaches Rosco's garbage can, a strong wind comes along and rips the letters out of his hand and carries them to the sidewalk. (See the grid below.) The wind continues to move them around.

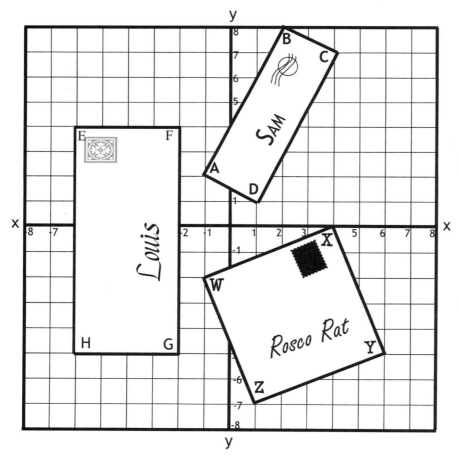

1. The wind flips the letter to Louis across line FG. Where will corner H be after the flip? (Give the coordinates.)

   _____ (        )

2. The wind rotates the letter to Sam clockwise 180° around corner D. Where will corner A be after the rotation?

   _____ (        )

3. The wind slides the letter to Rosco along the ground, moving it three spaces right and two spaces up. Where will corner Z be after the slide?

   _____ (        )

Name_____

# Tricky Math

Watch Rosco the Magnificent pull another great math trick out of his hat.
Read the steps, then see if you can repeat the trick.

- He pulls three numbers at random and forms a 3-digit number.
- He writes the number, then repeats the digits in the same order to get a 6-digit number.
- He divides the 6-digit number by 13.
- He divides the resulting number by 11.
- He divides that resulting number by 7.
- The final answer will ALWAYS be the original number.

### Example:

526

526,526

526,526 ÷ 13 = 40,502

40,502 ÷ 11 = 3,682

3,682 ÷ 7 = 526

TRY IT OUT THREE TIMES. CHOOSE A DIFFERENT
3-DIGIT NUMBER EACH TIME. FOLLOW THE STEPS.

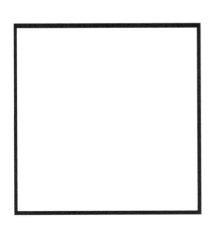

Name_____

# The Interrupted Blink

I'M ALL BLINKED OUT!

Boomerang and a group of cats were chosen to participate in a scientific study on cat blinks. Some curious scientists wanted to find out how often a cat blinks its eyes!

The scientists counted the blinks of all the cats five hours a day for a full week. During this time, they counted a total of **63,000** blinks.

Using their sharp math skills, the scientists calculated that each cat blinked an average of five times per minute.

**A.** How many cats participated in the study with Boomerang?

**B.** Later, Boomerang conducted his own study. He kept his lids closed five minutes for each blink. How many times would he probably blink in the eight hours he was awake that day?

Name_____

76

# Trouble on the Cheese Line

Rosco headed out from his garbage can home (A) toward his favorite restaurant, the Cheese Palace (B).

When he had walked 1000 feet, *exactly halfway* along the path from A to B, he heard a snore. Meatball, the guard dog, blocked the way! In a flash, Rosco decided he would choose another route to his destination. He hurried back to corner A (see his diagram) and walked instead from A to C (Boomerang's home). From there, he walked 1600 feet from point C to the restaurant at point B. He loaded the cheese and headed home.

Rosco decided to avoid returning on route BA (where the dog still snored) and took the long way around from B to C to A. He was exhausted when he got home!

HOW FAR DID ROSCO WALK
ON HIS TRIP TO AND FROM
THE RESTAURANT?

CHEESE PALACE

Name_____

# Pick-Up Stick Puzzler

In this game, the challenge is to pick up each stick without disturbing the other sticks. As Rosco Rat examines the pile, you do the same. Mentally choose the order in which the sticks should be picked up without moving other sticks.

Describe your steps by writing the colors of the sticks in the order you would pick them up.

ANOTHER STICK-Y SITUATION!

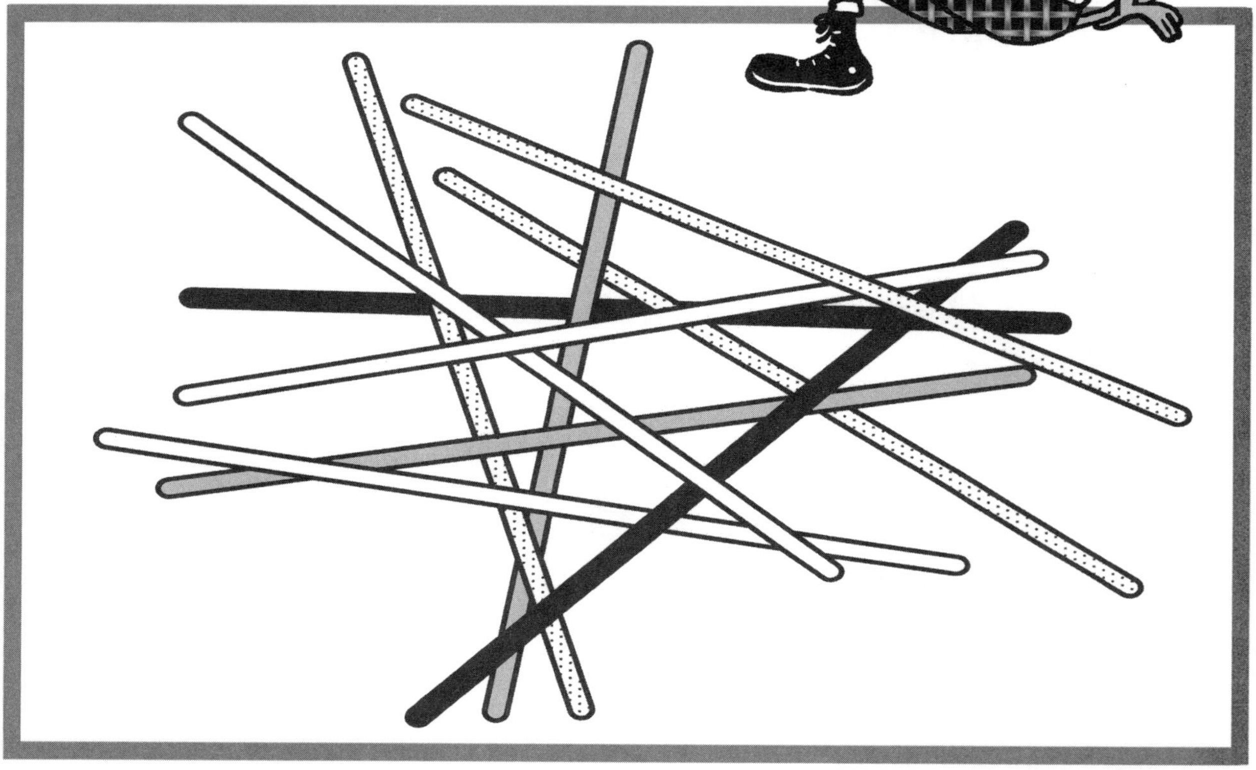

| black | gray |
| dots | white |

1._____     5._____     9._____

2._____     6._____     10._____

3._____     7._____

4._____     8._____

Name_____

78

# Costly Messages

The cell phone is Rosco's constant companion. He's hooked on texting, and those messages can get rather expensive. The cost of messages he sends and receives is calculated in an unusual way.

Examine the samples to figure out the pattern for the charges.

THEN FOLLOW THE COST PATTERN TO FIND THE VALUE OF EACH MESSAGE BELOW. RANK THEM 1 TO 8 IN ORDER OF VALUE, WITH 1 BEING THE LEAST EXPENSIVE.

ASK HR
2 D
DNC
52¢

NOT
ME
19¢

w8 4
Inch
45¢

YGTBK
25¢

TTYL
20¢

_____ JK, CUL8R
_____ BRNG PZA
_____ 2 L8 4 LNCH
_____ GT 2 RN
_____ WHRS D PRTE
_____ M SO BORD
_____ WL THR B DONUTS
_____ I H8 MNDAZ

Name_____

# Unfinished Recipes

Chef Portia is planning a dinner party for 30 of her most intimate friends. When she learns that Rosco Rat and his entire clan plan to attend, she increases the recipe to make sure there will be enough mozzarella treats for her cheese-loving guests.

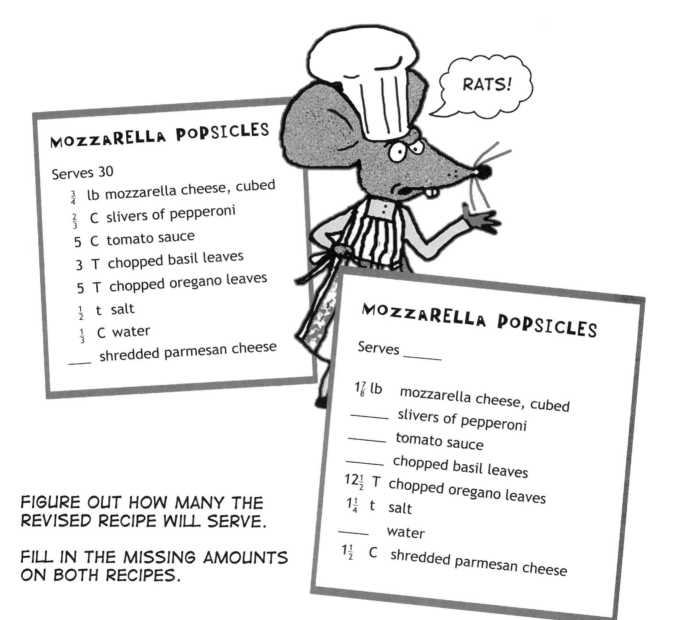

RATS!

### MOZZARELLA POPSICLES

Serves 30

- $\frac{3}{4}$ lb mozzarella cheese, cubed
- $\frac{2}{3}$ C slivers of pepperoni
- 5 C tomato sauce
- 3 T chopped basil leaves
- 5 T chopped oregano leaves
- $\frac{1}{2}$ t salt
- $\frac{1}{3}$ C water
- _____ shredded parmesan cheese

### MOZZARELLA POPSICLES

Serves _____

- $1\frac{7}{8}$ lb mozzarella cheese, cubed
- _____ slivers of pepperoni
- _____ tomato sauce
- _____ chopped basil leaves
- $12\frac{1}{2}$ T chopped oregano leaves
- $1\frac{1}{4}$ t salt
- _____ water
- $1\frac{1}{2}$ C shredded parmesan cheese

**FIGURE OUT HOW MANY THE REVISED RECIPE WILL SERVE.**

**FILL IN THE MISSING AMOUNTS ON BOTH RECIPES.**

Name_____

80

# What the Wizard Knows

Rosco fancies himself a bit of a wizard at solving math puzzles, but he's having trouble with this one. See if you can be a wizard and solve it for him.

Match the clues to the numbers. On the line before each clue, write the puzzle location of the number that answers the clue. For instance, write 6-D (6 Down) or 4-A (4 Across).

Watch out! This puzzle is tricky. A few digits are missing. You'll have to figure out what those are, and fill them in.

UH, OH!
BRAIN-FREEZE!

| ¹1 | | ²9 | 6 | ³8 | 0 | | |
| 0 | | | | | | | |
| ⁴ | 7 | 0 | 0 | 0 | | | ⁵1 |
| 4 | | | | 0 | | ⁶1 | 6 |
| | | | ⁷1 | 0 | 0 | 0 | 0 |
| | | | 1 | | | 0 | |
| | ⁸1 | 8 | 5 | | | ⁹8 | 0 |
| ¹⁰9 | 0 | | 2 | | | | |
| | 4 | | | | | | |

**CLUES:** Find the number of . . .

_____ a. toes on two human octets
_____ b. zeros in 100 googols
_____ c. meters in a nautical mile
_____ d. wings on a score of dragonflies
_____ e. legs on 12 dozen arachnids
_____ f. decades in nine centuries
_____ g. square yards in two acres
_____ h. millimeters in 27 meters
_____ i. hours in three fortnights
_____ j. pints in a full 13-gallon tub
_____ k. noses on 16 human octogenarians
_____ l. tablespoons in four gallons
_____ m. yards in 50 miles

Name_____

Math Conundrums—Learning Adventures Series

# The Final Darts

Rosco's dart board is one of a kind. He threw six darts. (See them on the target.)
Later, he tossed three more darts for a final total score of 402.

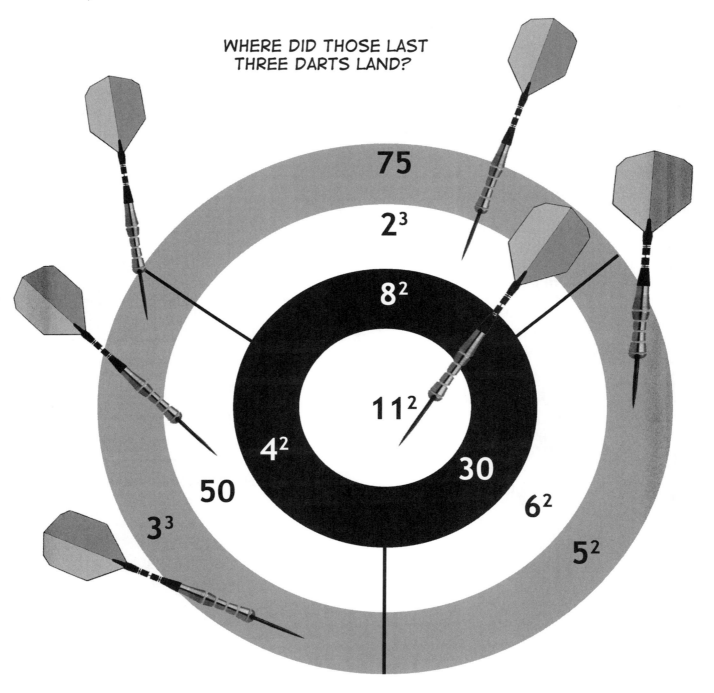

WHERE DID THOSE LAST
THREE DARTS LAND?

Name_____

# The Pirate's Log

- Pirate Rosco hit the deck of his boat, *The Grey Oyster*, and worked to get her ready to sail. He set sail two hours and fifteen minutes later from Fire Island.

- It took twelve hours and forty-five minutes to reach the harbor at Doubloon Bay.

- For four hours, Rosco anchored the ship and swabbed the decks.

- He polished the plank for another two hours.

- With the boat in shipshape condition, he settled down to groom his parrot, Gabby. This took one hour and forty-five minutes. He spent another two hours trying to teach new words to the parrot.

- When it was time to leave, Rosco rowed the dinghy to shore alone. This took ten minutes.

- It took another twenty-five minutes to hike to the cave where his ancestor supposedly stashed his treasure. Eureka! He found the booty. It took fifty-five minutes to drag the chest to the dinghy and row to the ship.

- Rosco spent three hours counting (and eating) the treasure of well-aged, exotic cheeses he found in the chest. Then he slept for ten hours.

- When he awoke, he set sail for the ten-hour trip to Schooner Bay.

- *The Grey Oyster* arrived in Schooner Bay on Thursday at 9:15 PM.

One of Rosco's ancestors was the captain of a pirate ship! When Rosco found the Captain's log, he decided to re-enact One-eyed Ratbeard's last voyage precisely. (And maybe find some treasure?)

LUCKILY, I FIT INTO GREAT UNCLE RATBEARD'S CLOTHES.

Study the timeline and answer these questions:

A. WHEN DID ROSCO SET SAIL FROM FIRE ISLAND?

B. WHAT TIME (AND DAY) DID THE PIRATE FINISH GROOMING THE PARROT?

Name_____

# Who's Next?

These patients were all mistakenly scheduled to see the dentist on the same day at the time. Someone's going to have to figure out a logical order for seeing them.

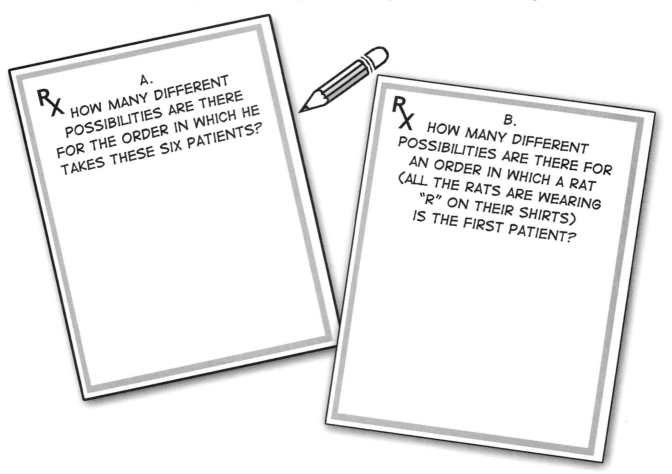

**A.** HOW MANY DIFFERENT POSSIBILITIES ARE THERE FOR THE ORDER IN WHICH HE TAKES THESE SIX PATIENTS?

**B.** HOW MANY DIFFERENT POSSIBILITIES ARE THERE FOR AN ORDER IN WHICH A RAT (ALL THE RATS ARE WEARING "R" ON THEIR SHIRTS) IS THE FIRST PATIENT?

Name_____

84

Math Conundrum #76

# Conundrum on the Slopes

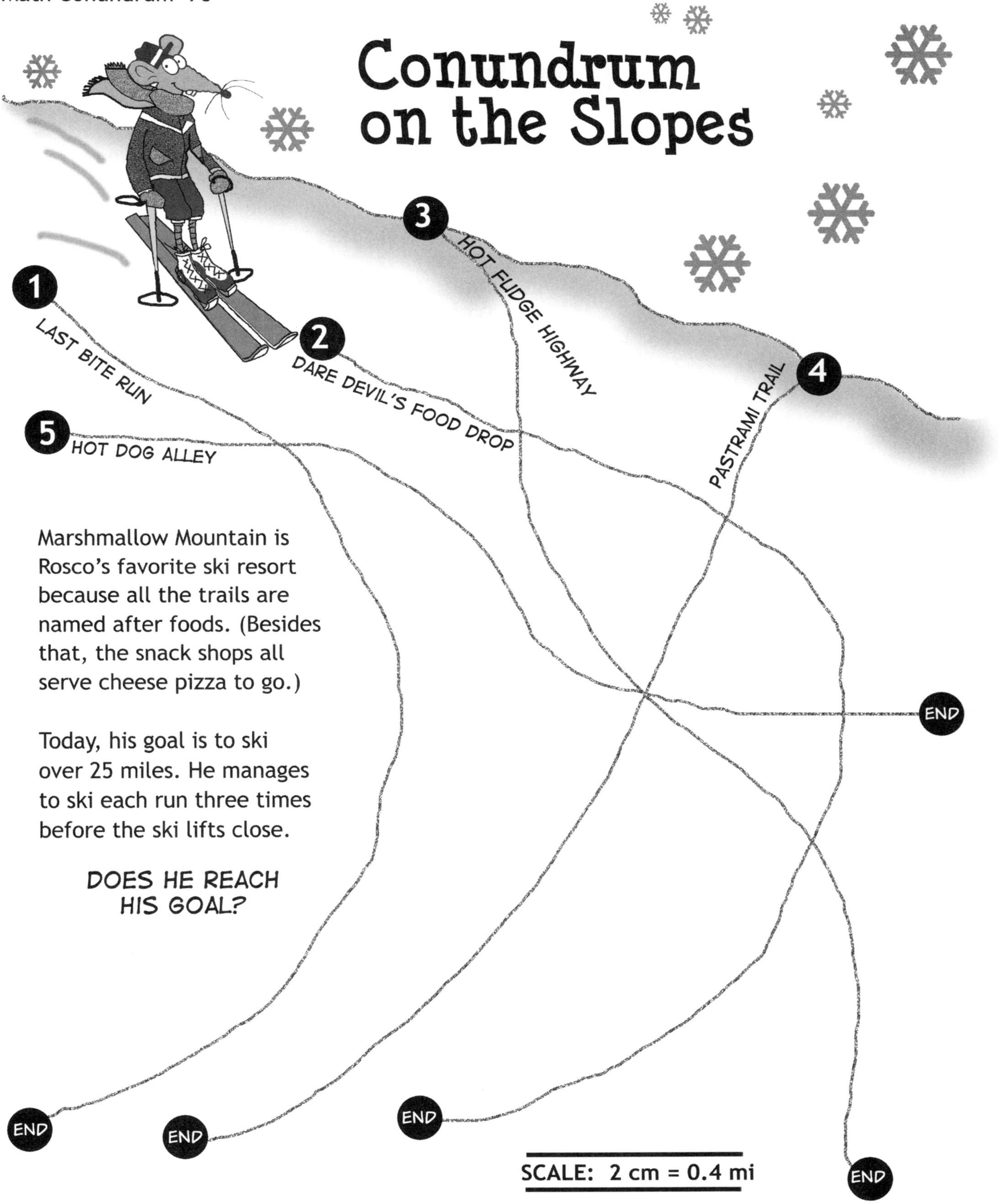

**3** HOT FUDGE HIGHWAY

**1** LAST BITE RUN

**2** DARE DEVIL'S FOOD DROP

**4** PASTRAMI TRAIL

**5** HOT DOG ALLEY

Marshmallow Mountain is
Rosco's favorite ski resort
because all the trails are
named after foods. (Besides
that, the snack shops all
serve cheese pizza to go.)

Today, his goal is to ski
over 25 miles. He manages
to ski each run three times
before the ski lifts close.

**DOES HE REACH
HIS GOAL?**

END

END · END · END · END

SCALE: 2 cm = 0.4 mi

Name_____

# The View from Space

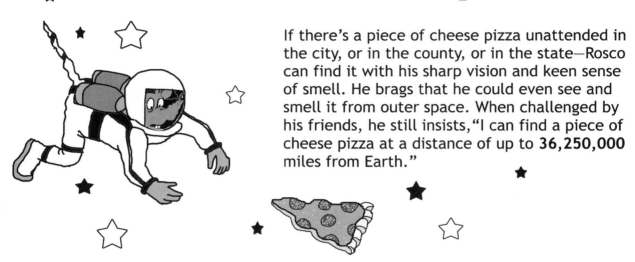

If there's a piece of cheese pizza unattended in the city, or in the county, or in the state—Rosco can find it with his sharp vision and keen sense of smell. He brags that he could even see and smell it from outer space. When challenged by his friends, he still insists, "I can find a piece of cheese pizza at a distance of up to **36,250,000** miles from Earth."

**IF ROSCO IS NOT EXAGGERATING, FROM WHICH OF THESE DISTANCES (IN MILES) COULD HE SEE THE PIZZA SLICE? (CIRCLE THEM.)**

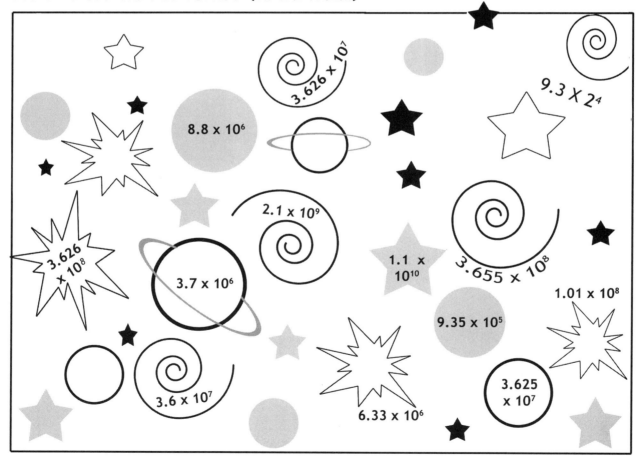

$3.626 \times 10^7$

$9.3 \times 2^4$

$8.8 \times 10^6$

$2.1 \times 10^9$

$3.626 \times 10^8$

$3.7 \times 10^6$

$1.1 \times 10^{10}$

$3.655 \times 10^8$

$1.01 \times 10^8$

$9.35 \times 10^5$

$3.6 \times 10^7$

$6.33 \times 10^6$

$3.625 \times 10^7$

Name_____

# Just Plane Logic

Rosco won a contest! The prize is four individual round-trip plane rides, one for himself and three friends. The eager travelers Rosco, Boomerang, Portia, and Meatball have each chosen to visit four different U.S. cities.

*FOLLOW THE CLUES AND USE LOGIC TO FIGURE OUT WHO FLIES TO ALBUQUERQUE.*

## CLUES:

Portia does not like boats.

Meatball did not shop for shoes or cheese.

The one who went to Boston was not on a shoe shopping trip.

Boomerang did not take a trip to buy exotic cheeses.

Rosco has never been (or intends to be) west of the Mississippi River.

The one who went to Chattanooga was looking for cheese.

Rosco went to Chattanooga.

Rosco did not go on a trip to visit a cousin.

The passenger who went to Milwaukee did so to board a yacht on Lake Michigan.

The passenger who went to Albuquerque was not looking for cheese.

Boomerang did not go to Milwaukee or Boston.

Name_____

# Fun on a Tight Budget

Riding the jet ski is a blast—but Meatball knows it's not free. With gasoline at $4.00 a gallon, he finds that his favorite water sport is getting too expensive for his budget.

Then someone suggests that he might stretch his money by riding the jet ski at a slower speed. This would not be a speed-demon's first option, but he decides to do the math.

At his usual speed of 30 mph, he uses a gallon of gas every 25 minutes of skiing. When he reduces the speed to an average of 20 mph, a gallon lasts for 40 minutes.

IF HE JET SKIS FOR THREE HOURS WITHOUT STOPPING, HOW MUCH MONEY CAN MEATBALL SAVE IN THE COST OF GAS IF HE REDUCES HIS SPEED TO 20 MPH?

Name_____

# Translate the Plates

Boomerang is awed by the fancy cars in Lester Fatcat's garage. He wonders what it would feel like to take a ride in one of them.

The license plates on the cars are not only clever; they contain coded information about the values of the cars. Break the code to find the answer to this question:

WHAT IS THE DIFFERENCE BETWEEN THE MOST VALUABLE CAR AND THE LEAST VALUABLE CAR?

**Each letter has the value of its opposite in the alphabet.**

**C, the third letter, has a value of X (the third letter from the end of the alphabet). X is the 24th letter, so C is worth $24. The value of X, then is $3.**

**Likewise K (the 12th letter) has a value of P (12th from the end but 16th from the beginning). K = $16 and P = $12.**

1. Translate each plate into full words.

2. Use the code to find the dollar value for each letter.

3. Find the sum of the letter values for each license plate.

4. The value of the plate is $\frac{1}{60}$ of the value of the car. Find the value of each car.

Name_____

# Star Power

Rosco is a great movie fan. Whenever he can sneak his way into a movie theater, he'll take the opportunity to scavenge for popcorn and catch a good story. So you can imagine his delight when he was recruited for a role in the latest sequel to *Rats of the Caribbean*! The movie took in $198,000,000 worldwide.

I'M READY FOR MY CLOSE-UP, MR. DeVARMINT.

- He required a one-hour break for every two hours of work. (It's hard for rats to stay put for too long at one time!)

- For every two hours of work, he required three large boxes of popcorn and a half hour break to eat them.

- He required 30% of the total intake of money for the movie.

Rosco was present at the movie location five days a week, seven hours a day, for twelve weeks.

WHAT WAS ROSCO'S AVERAGE RATE OF PAY PER HOUR FOR THE TIME HE ACTUALLY WORKED? *(Eating and sleeping were not included in the definition of actual work.)*

90

Name_____

# A Precarious Dance

Somehow Boomerang convinced Portia Mouse to take dance lessons with him. It ought to be easy, he told her—using the dance pattern on the floor.

Trace a safe path for these amateurs to use during dance practice.

Begin at the square with the START label.

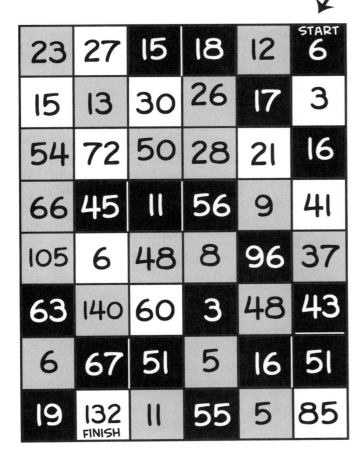

The pair can move from square to square by going up, down, left, or right, but not diagonally. Furthermore, they can only move to a square of the same color OR to a square with a number that shares a multiple >3 with the previous number.

KEEP THEM MOVING ACROSS THE FLOOR TO THE SQUARE WITH THE FINISH LABEL. DRAW A RED LINE AS YOU GO TO MARK THEIR SAFE PATH.

Name_____

# A Literary Lunch

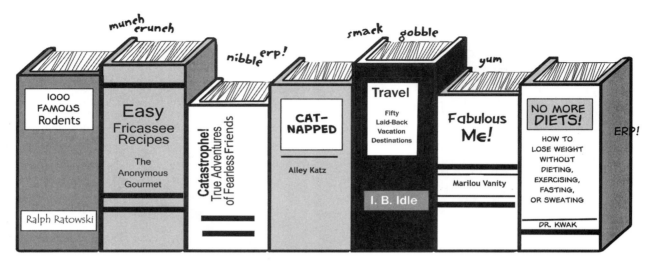

Rosco Rat reads contentedly, unaware that a bookworm has also decided to devour some knowledge. It has secretly begun to eat through some books.

The front and back covers of each book are **one centimeter** thick. The total thickness of each volume (including covers) is **seven centimeters.**

The bookworm intends to eat through the front cover of the first book on the left and move in a straight line through the back cover of the last book, eating all the way. Perhaps he also reads as he goes.

**HOW FAR WILL THE BOOKWORM HAVE TO TRAVEL ON THIS EATING JOURNEY?**

Name_____

92

# Reflections and Deceptions

LOOKIN' FINE!

Rosco is pleased with his reflection!
He can see the world reflected in his mirror, too.

Some images from the street are shown below.
See if you can correctly identify the reflected image
of the old car, the bicyclist, and the garbage can.

---

CIRCLE EXAMPLES THAT COULD BE REFLECTIONS OF A, B, OR C.

Name_____

# The Missing Scores

It takes skill to knock down all the pins in a bowling game. It also takes skill to keep score! Rosco has bowled a pretty good game, but he's been confused about some of the score keeping.

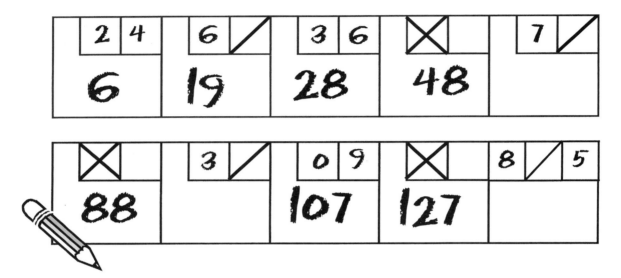

**In bowling, there are ten frames.**
In each frame, a bowler gets two throws to knock down the ten pins. Each pin down is worth one point. The points in each frame get added to those in the previous frame.

**If it takes two throws of the ball** to knock down all ten, Rosco gets a SPARE (marked with one diagonal line). With a spare, he is able to add the value of the NEXT throw to the ten points for that frame.

**If Rosco knocks down all ten pins** with the first throw, he gets a STRIKE (marked with an X). With a strike, he is able to add the value of the next TWO throws to the ten points for that frame.

**If a bowler gets a spare or a strike** in the final frame, he can throw the ball one or two more times, respectively, to get the score.

Rosco wrote the correct numbers of pins knocked down for each frame. But he couldn't figure out the score in three of the frames.

FILL IN THE MISSING SCORES.

Name_____

# Sandwiches by Chance

Portia Mouse has loaded a picnic basket with food for a party of finicky eaters. She packed eight different kinds of sandwiches to please every palate, but unfortunately, she forgot to label them.

Rosco Rat doesn't really care. He likes everything! He pulls out a sandwich.

COME AND GET IT!

**The number and kind of sandwiches in the basket are:**

6 PEANUT BUTTER AND JELLY

2 ROAST BEEF AND SWISS CHEESE

5 TUNA AND SALAMI

4 BANANA AND PEANUT BUTTER

2 SALAMI AND CHEDDAR CHEESE

2 CREAM CHEESE AND JELLY

3 TUNA AND SWISS CHEESE

4 PEANUT BUTTER, TUNA, AND CREAM CHEESE

## WHICH IS GREATER?

**A.** the odds in favor of getting a sandwich with cheese but no peanut butter

   *OR*

**B.** the odds against getting a sandwich with tuna, salami, or cheese

Name_____

   Math Conundrums—Learning Adventures Series

# A Pizza Perplexity

Rosco challenges Boomerang to cut the pizza into six slices of equal size and shape. Moreover, he wants each piece to have exactly the same number of salami slices.

Can the cat do it? How?

DRAW ON THE PIZZA TO SHOW HOW BOOMERANG CAN MEET ROSCO'S CHALLENGE!

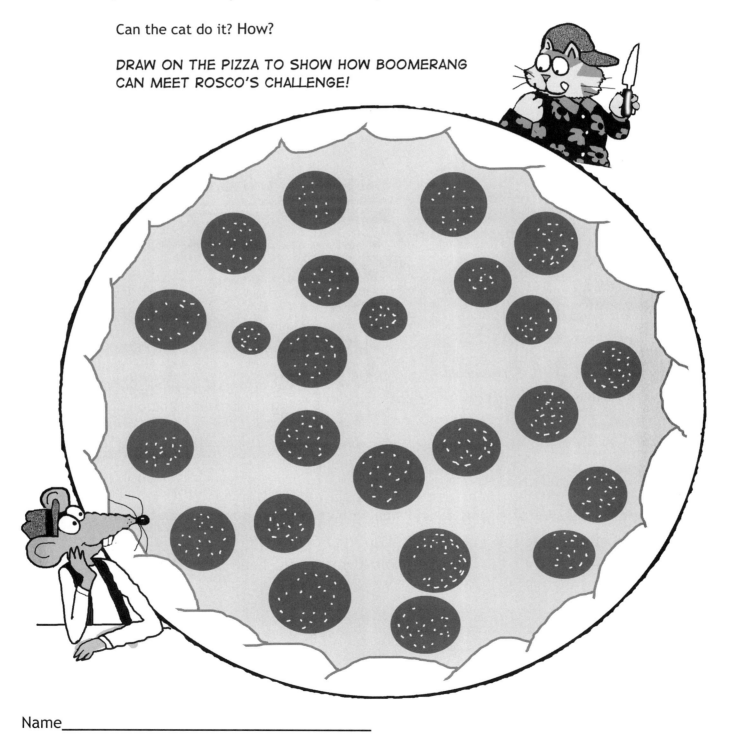

Name_____

# She's a Real Rat!

Rosco arrived at the hospital to see his newborn niece. The babies all had numbers on them, and they all looked identical! How was Rosco going to tell which one was his niece?

64,083    521,225    4882    651,026

1,212,122    6816

### HERE'S HOW TO TELL!

Rosco's niece is wearing a number:

- that is not a prime number
- that has three even digits other than zero
- whose digits have a product <550
- that is not a palindrome
- that is not divisible by 12
- in which one digit or consecutive pair of digits is the double of another digit

360,368    76,214    800,816    324,200

Name_____

# High Hopes

Hiding around a corner, Rosco notices that a worker at The City Center Grille has just loaded the trash can with leftovers. It looks as if customers asked for their uneaten food to be boxed to go, and then walked away—forgetting to grab the containers. Rosco is hoping to find some cheesy leftovers in these little boxes.

The can contains 24 containers. Six contain leftover cheeseburgers. Three contain leftover cheese fries. Six contain leftover lime cheesecake. The rest contain vegan chile (no animal products in this).

Rosco reaches in and grabs one container.

    A. WHAT IS THE PROBABILITY THAT IT WILL NOT CONTAIN ANY CHEESE?

    B. WHAT IS THE PROBABILITY THAT IT WILL CONTAIN CHEESECAKE?

Assume that the first container held cheese fries. Rosco gobbles them up, tosses the container aside, and grabs another container from the trash can.

    C. WHAT IS THE PROBABILITY THAT THIS WILL CONTAIN A DISH THAT HAS CHEESE?

    D. WHAT IS THE PROBABILITY THAT THIS WILL CONTAIN CHEESE FRIES?

    E. WHAT IS THE PROBABILITY THAT THIS WILL CONTAIN A CHEESEBURGER?

Name_____

98

# Blisters, Anyone?

Among Rosco's many talents is his ability to dance, run, or walk on his hands for long spells of time. It really is quite amazing.

Rosco usually does some activity on his hands every day.
Here is his schedule for last week:

| SUNDAY | He danced on his hands for 3 hours and 10 minutes. |

| MONDAY | He danced on his hands for twice the time as Sunday. |

| TUESDAY | He walked on his hands for 4 hours and 6 minutes. |

| WEDNESDAY | He ran on his hands for ¾ hour in the morning and the same amount of time again in the afternoon. |

| THURSDAY | He danced again on his hands. |

| FRIDAY | His blisters were so bad that he took the day off. |

| SATURDAY | He danced on his hands for 75 minutes in the morning and the same amount of time again in the afternoon. |

DURING THE WEEK, ROSCO SPENT A TOTAL OF 19 HOURS
AND 6 MINUTES ON HIS HANDS. HOW LONG DID HE DANCE
ON HIS HANDS ON THURSDAY?

Name_____

Name _____ Date _____

**1.** Rosco makes the rounds of his favorite food haunts: the dumpster behind Hank's Hot Dog Hut, the back door of Joe's Pizzaria, the picnic tables in Rand Park, the trash can at Puck's Doughnuts, and the Catskill High School cafeteria. If he visits these in a different order each day, how many days will it take before he'll run out of possibilities for a different order?

**2.** Meatball chased cats every day last week except Tuesday—for a total of 59 during the week. On Monday, he chased one-third the number that he chased on Sunday. On Wednesday, he chased twice as many as on Monday. He chased 12 on Thursday and 12 on Friday. On Saturday, he chased the same number as on Monday. How many did he chase on Sunday?

**3.** Some prankster put Rosco in a tough predicament. A train is 170 miles away. Rosco has $2\frac{1}{2}$ hours before the train arrives. How fast is the train traveling?

**4.** Which of the following equations can be used to solve the problem below?

a. $14 = 2x + 3x - x$

b. $x + \frac{1}{2}x + \frac{1}{6}x + \frac{2}{3}x = 14$

c. $14 - \frac{1}{3} - \frac{1}{2} - \frac{2}{3} = x$

d. $4x - 14 = S$

*Four friends of Rosco's have ages that total 14. Arlo is half of Sal's age. Lucas is $\frac{1}{3}$ of Arlo's age. Rene is $\frac{2}{3}$ of Sal's age. How old is Sal?*

**5.** Portia Mouse stashed away 18 crumbles of cheese in an hour. If she can continue at this rate, how long will it take her to stash 63 crumbles?

**6.** Which of Rosco's containers can hold more root beer?

a. a cylinder with a 4-inch diameter and 5-inch height

b. a cone with a 3-inch radius and a 4-inch height

c. a rectangular prism with a height of 5 inches and a 3- by 4-inch base

**7.** Rosco and his friends ate a whole round pizza that was 2 centimeters thick with a total volume of 2512 cubic centimeters. What was the diameter of the pizza?

**8.** This month, Rosco's part-time movie career lands him a role as a robber. As he slinks away into the night, two coins fall out of a hole in the bag. The bag held lots of cheese and four kinds of coins: quarters, dimes, nickels, and pennies. How many different combinations of two coins could possibly be left behind on the ground?

**9.** The bases are loaded in a neighborhood baseball game, and a fourth member of the team is at bat. Rosco is not on first. Meatball is one base closer to scoring than Boomerang. Portia is on a base that is between Rosco and Meatball. Portia is not on first base. Who's the batter?

**10.** Rosco ate an amount of macaroni and cheese (measured in pounds) represented by this expression: $6x + (-20 - 12)$. Translate the mathematical expression into words.

**11.** A rat catcher spent many unsuccessful hours trying to ensnare Rosco. Translate these words into a mathematical expression that represents the amount of time.

NINE TIMES A NUMBER SQUARED DIVIDED BY THE PRODUCT OF FOUR AND FIVE

**12.** What is missing from this problem?

_____

_____

_____

_____

_____

*When Boomerang Cat asked Portia to dance, she refused 96% of his requests. How many times did they dance?*

**13.** Which of the
following equations
represents a line
connecting all the
slices of pizza
on the grid?

    a.   y = x + 3

    b.   y = 2x + 1

    c.   x = −y

    d.   y = x − 3

    e.   x = 1 − y

    f.   x = −4y

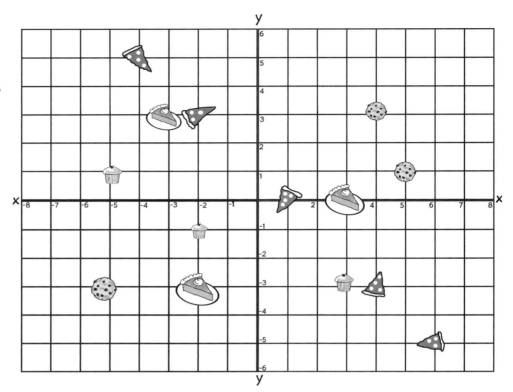

**14.** Boomerang's pizza is sliced into
12 slices. The radius of the pizza is
6 inches. What is the area of the
top of one slice? (Circle the best
estimate.)

    a.   12 in.²

    b.   10 in.²

    c.   8 in.²

    d.   120 in.²

**15.** Rosco can visit all five of his
favorite food locations in one hour.
Fifteen minutes are spent eating.
He moves the rest of the hour. The
total distance he travels on his
route is 10.5 miles. What is his
rate of travel?

**16.** Rosco swats (and squishes) 42 flies
(six legs each) and 22 spiders (eight
legs each). What is the ratio of
squished spider legs to squished fly
legs (in lowest terms)?

**17.** Portia Mouse's four cousins are three
years apart in age. How many of
their ages could be odd numbers?

**18.** The ages of the cousins (in problem
17) total 18 years. How old is the
oldest of the four?

         

WHACK!

**19.** Meatball hits 20% of his tennis shots out of the court into the trees. He hits 25% out of bounds to the right. He hits 5% out of bounds to the left. He hits 10% directly into his unlucky opponent. Meatball hits the rest of the shots into the net. Out of a total of 60 shots, how many does he hit into the net?

**20.** Rosco shares a fat, juicy sausage with five friends. Boomerang gets $\frac{5}{30}$. Portia gets $\frac{2}{15}$. Meatball gets $\frac{3}{10}$. Arlo gets $\frac{4}{20}$, and Rosco is left with $\frac{1}{5}$. Which two friends get the same amount of sausage?

   a.  Meatball and Portia

   b.  Portia and Boomerang

   c.  Meatball and Arlo

   d.  Boomerang and Rosco

   e.  Rosco and Arlo

   f.  Portia and Meatball

   g.  Meatball and Boomerang

**21.** Which equation will solve the problem below?

   a.  $30x + 10x = 148$

   b.  $x = 30x - 3x + 148$

   c.  $148 - x(30 - 3 - 10) = x$

   d.  $17x + 10(2x) = 148$

The cheese factory threw away a total of 148 pounds of cheese in April—tossing cheese each day but April 24 to 26. The amount thrown out each of the last ten days was twice that of the other days. How many pounds were thrown out on April 16?

The garbage can behind the Cat's Tail Café is a favorite spot for Rosco's scavenging trips. Today the can contains 28 cheeseburgers, 14 slices of pizza, 30 cupcakes, and 8 pastrami sandwiches. Rosco reaches in and grabs one item.

**22.** What is the probability that it will be a cupcake?

**23.** What is the probability that it will be a cheeseburger?

**24.** What is the probability that it will be a sandwich?

**25.** What is the probability that it will not be a slice of pizza?

**26.** A huge wedding picnic ended at 5:35 p.m. after seven hours and fifty minutes of celebration. Rosco and several of his rat friends arrived half-way through the party to snap up scraps of food.

 a. What time did the picnic begin?

 b. What information in the problem is not necessary for solving the problem? (Circle it.)

**27.** The magician has nine rabbits, four owls, three hedgehogs, and four parakeets in his hat. He pulls out a hedgehog on his first reach.

 a. What is the probability that he will grab another hedgehog on his second try?

 b. If he does get a hedgehog the second time, what is the probability that he will grab a parakeet on his third try?

**28.** In a recent trip to the gym, Rosco ran 33.6 minutes on the treadmill. This took up 21% of his gym time. How long did Rosco spend at the gym?

 a. 2 hours

 b. 2½ hours

 c. 2 hours, 6 minutes

 d. 79 minutes

 e. 2 hours, 40 minutes

 f. none of the above

**29.** The mouse smells a juicy slice of pizza. Then she spies a plump doughnut. How much further will she have to travel if she picks up the doughnut on her way to the pizza slice than if she heads straight to the pizza? (She will stay on the path.)

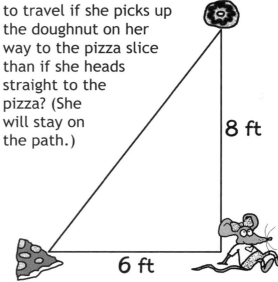

**8 ft**

**6 ft**

**30.** A rat brags that she has avoided this many traps: the product of twelve times a number squared and ten times another number squared. Which expression matches her claim?

 a. $(12x^2)\ (10y^2)$

 b. $(12x^2)\ (10x^2)$

 c. $12x^2 + 10y^2$

 d. $(10)\ (12)\ (x^2)$

**31.** Rosco dreams of traveling $9.99 \times 10^7$ miles into space. Boomerang dreams of traveling $1.6 \times 10^8$ miles into space. Whose dreams take him the farthest?

**32.** Cat #1 prowled the streets for $3\frac{3}{4}$ hours. Cat #2 prowled for 188 minutes. Cat #3 prowled for 13,510 seconds. Which cat prowled longest?

**33.** Portia is determined to improve her soccer skills. She practices about 190 minutes a day, every day for ten months. Use mental math to estimate the amount of practice in hours.

**34.** It is said that rats will desert a sinking ship. Five rat friends (Len, Ren, Sven, Jen, and Ben) sense that a boat is sinking. They leap off and swim for shore. Len jumps before Ben but after Sven. Jen is three jumpers behind Ren. Sven jumps just ahead of Len. Who is the last jumper?

**35.** Meatball loves chocolate milk. He has a choice of a 4-liter jug full of chocolate milk or a jug that is filled with 12 pints. Which container should he choose?

**36.** Rosco enjoys this piece of cheese that is a triangular prism in shape. It has a height of 4 inches and a base that is a triangle with a 3-inch width and a 6-inch height. But the cheese has holes! One-third of the cheese is air! How much cheese will Rosco enjoy if he eats it all?

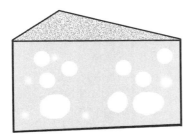

**37.** A rat speeds through the underground sewers, covering 2.7 miles in 45 minutes. If he can continue at this rate, how far can he travel in 3 hours?

**38.** Rosco and his friend Arlo spend a good bit of time swatting bothersome flies and bees. Yesterday Arlo swatted one more than half as many as Rosco. Rosco swatted a number that has two different even digits and is greater than 20 but less than 30. How many did Arlo swat? Find at least two different answers.

**39.** A spider crawls around one base of a 15-cm tall rectangular prism block of cheese. The base of the cheese is 10 cm wide, and the cheese has a volume of 1200 cm$^3$. How far will the spider travel on one trip around the edges of one base?

**40.** In his scavenging trips, Rosco often finds leftover doughnuts. The trouble is, ants sometimes get to the doughnuts before he does. To predict how many of the next 1800 doughnuts will be ant-infested, Rosco takes a random sampling of 150. Of these, 17 have ants. In how many of the total 1800 can he expect to find ants?

# Conundrum Record-Keeping Chart  Name_____

**Directions:** When you have completed the Conundrum, write X over the number. When you are confident that you are comfortable with the concepts and processes used in the Conundrum, write X in the *Yes!* column.

| C-# | Title | YES! | C-# | Title | YES! | C-# | Title | YES! |
|---|---|---|---|---|---|---|---|---|
| 1 | Clever Scavenger | | 31 | Football Fanatics | | 61 | To Swat . . . | |
| 2 | Pizza Mix-Up | | 32 | Coin Confusion | | 62 | Edible Geometry | |
| 3 | Matter of Age | | 33 | Lost in Space | | 63 | Headed for . . . | |
| 4 | Confusion . . . | | 34 | Diving Dilemma | | 64 | Cheeses . . . | |
| 5 | Money . . . | | 35 | Take a Break | | 65 | Mail on the Move | |
| 6 | Tasty Endeavor | | 36 | The Race . . . | | 66 | Tricky Math | |
| 7 | Favorite Finds | | 37 | Pizza Probabilities | | 67 | Interrupted Blink | |
| 8 | Filled to Capacity | | 38 | Hang Ten | | 68 | Trouble . . . | |
| 9 | Bruised . . . | | 39 | Many Right . . . | | 69 | Pick Up Stick . . . | |
| 10 | Who's on . . . | | 40 | Milkshake Metrics | | 70 | Costly . . . | |
| 11 | Rescue at Sea | | 41 | Honeycomb . . . | | 71 | Unfinished . . . | |
| 12 | Flying Spheres | | 42 | Strange Laws | | 72 | What the Wizard . . . | |
| 13 | Right Combination | | 43 | An Exercise . . . | | 73 | Final Dart | |
| 14 | Celestial . . . | | 44 | Missing Out | | 74 | Pirate's Log | |
| 15 | Daily Five | | 45 | Mac & Cheese . . . | | 75 | Who's Next? | |
| 16 | Time Matters | | 46 | Key Question | | 76 | Conundrum . . . | |
| 17 | Indigestion . . . | | 47 | Against the Flow | | 77 | View from Space | |
| 18 | Painter's . . . | | 48 | Golf Trivia | | 78 | Just Plane . . . | |
| 19 | Tennis Troubles | | 49 | Music Makes . . . | | 79 | Fun on a . . . | |
| 20 | Who Won . . . | | 50 | The One That . . . | | 80 | Translate the Plates | |
| 21 | Whisker . . . | | 51 | Too Much . . . | | 81 | Star Power | |
| 22 | Watch Out . . . | | 52 | Where Did . . . | | 82 | Precarious Dance | |
| 23 | Toothpick Puzzler | | 53 | Follow Your Nose | | 83 | Literary Lunch | |
| 24 | Parachute . . . | | 54 | Handshakes . . . | | 84 | Reflections . . . | |
| 25 | Underwater Lunch | | 55 | Laundry Quandary | | 85 | Missing Scores | |
| 26 | Salty Solution | | 56 | Bring on the . . . | | 86 | Sandwiches . . . | |
| 27 | Must Be Magic | | 57 | Picking Up Speed | | 87 | Pizza . . . | |
| 28 | Up With Raisins | | 58 | On the Edge | | 88 | She's a Real . . . | |
| 29 | Sloppy Eating | | 59 | Good News | | 89 | High Hopes | |
| 30 | What's the . . . | | 60 | Puzzling . . . | | 90 | Blisters, Anyone? | |

# Problem-Solving Strategies

*A problem-solving strategy is a method for approaching and solving a problem. There are many different ways to solve problems. Different strategies fit well with different kinds of problems. One of the skills involved in sharp problem solving is the ability to choose a workable strategy for a particular problem. Here are some strategies to add to your toolbox for approaching problems.*

## Simplify the Problem

When a problem has lots of words, you can make it less complicated by re-wording it into a simpler question.

*The Problem:* Boomerang searched for a good deal on new dog collars. He wanted to spend no more than 20% of the $188 in coins and the $66 in bills that he had found and buried. When he goes shopping tomorrow, how much will he be willing to spend? *The Problem Simplified:* What is 20% of ($188 + $66)?

## Use Mental Math

Sometimes your head is the best strategy (and tool). You can think through a problem and come up with a solution without using any other tools. Mental math is great for time problems, estimation problems, and other simple calculations.

*The Problem:* Rosco begins his daily workout at 6:55 a.m. and finishes at 1:11 p.m. How long is his workout?

## Use Trial and Error

Sometimes the best approach is to try different solutions until you find one that works. Trial and Error is a good strategy for simple logic problems and for those sticky age problems.

*The Problem:* Al is five years younger than Sal. Two years ago, Al was 2/3 of Sal's age. In 3 years, Al will be 3/4 of Sal's age. In 20 years, the sum of their ages will be 69. How old is Al?

## Make a Model

For certain problems, it helps to actually see the object in the problem. This is the time to construct a model from paper, cardboard, toothpicks, marshmallows, straws, clay, or other common supplies.

*The Problem:* How many vertices are found on an octagonal prism?

## Guess and Check

For some problems, the best approach is to use all the good information you have to make a careful guess. After the guess, count or calculate to check your guess (if possible).

*The Problem:* How many gumballs are in that jar?

## Draw a Diagram, Table, or Graph

When you need to visualize a situation but it is not practical to build a model, draw a picture or diagram of the problem components. If there is a lot of data, put it into a table or graph so you can see the relationships between the numbers.

*The Problem:* Five swimmers race to a buoy, Nan is behind Dan but ahead of Van. Van is between Stan and Jan. Stan is behind Van. Who is in the lead?

## Write an Equation

When the problem has an unknown quantity, start by translating the words and numbers into an equation.

*The Problem:* 19 friends joined a hot dog-eating team. 2 dropped out each week for the first 3 weeks. Then 5 new members joined, giving the team 9 more members than last year. How many members were on the team last year?

## Estimate

An estimate is an approximate solution. If the problem asks for an approximate answer or uses words such as "about how much?" round the facts to get a ball-park answer.

*The Problem:* Rosco's soccer team needs plenty of towels for all their showers. 18 players shower after 6 practices and 2 games each week. The season is 11 weeks long. Will 2,000 clean towels be enough?

## Find a Common Element

If the facts in a problem include different units, start by converting all necessary information into the same unit—preferably the smallest common unit. When you have an answer in that unit, you might convert it to a larger unit.

*The Problem:* Rosco talked on his cell phone an hour on Sunday, 3 hours and 14 minutes on Monday, 39 minutes and 50 seconds on Tuesday, and 46 seconds each day on Wednesday through Saturday. How long did he talk last week?

## Choose a Formula

Sometimes a formula is a shortcut to a solution. The trick is to be sure to choose the right formula!

*The Problem:* A hungry cat ate a full box of cheese chips. The box was 10 cm wide, 25 cm long, and 15 cm tall. Each cubic centimeter in the box held 0.1 gram of chips. What was the total weight of the chips he ate?

## Work Backwards

When a problem has a missing fact somewhere in the middle or at the beginning of several items of data, start at the end and work backwards.

*The Problem:* A busy rat walked 30 minutes into town. His first stop was a school dumpster where he spent 9 minutes. Next, he walked 6 minutes to a pizza shop where he ate scraps for 10 minutes. He rested an hour, then walked to an ice cream stand and ate a cone in 3 minutes. He jogged home in 18 minutes, arriving home at 3:15 p.m. What time did he leave home?

## Write a Proportion

If a problem gives a ratio and asks for a solution at the same rate, set up a proportion to help find the solution.

*The Problem:* A total of eighty worms will race during a 2-day competition. Twenty worms started race #1. Six got injured during the race. At this rate, how many worms will get injured during the races?

## Extend a Pattern

If you can find a pattern in the data, you might be able to extend the pattern to solve the problem.

*The Problem:* Rosco's softball team won six games in a row. Here are the scores: Game One—3 to 1; Game Two—5 to 2; Game Three—7 to 3; Game Four—9 to 4. Infer the scores of Games Five and Six.

## Use Logic

When a problem requires you to use some information to make assumptions about other information, use *If . . . Then . . .* thinking to solve the problem.

*The Problem:* Each of four hikers has one of these ailments: blisters, headache, a sprained ankle, or ant bites. Maxie does not have ant bites. Neither Axle nor Sal has a headache. Sal does not have blisters. Neither does Maxie. Hal is limping. Who has blisters?

# Answer Keys

## The Conundrums, 1-90 (pages 10-99)

**Note:** Most of the problems, questions, or tasks within the Math Conundrums have specific solutions. However, students and others who pursue these may find different answers. Examine each answer to see if it is a reasonable response to the conundrum. Encourage the problem-solvers to give explanations or plausible arguments for their variant solutions. Encourage individual thinking. Discuss and compare responses.

**Conundrum #1 (pg 10)**
29,220 hours (Don't forget to take into account that 2004 and 2008 were leap years with 366 days.)

**Conundrum #2 (pg 11)**
5

**Conundrum #3 (pg 12)**
10 years difference
(Portia—4; Boomerang—6; Miles—2; Meatball—12)

**Conundrum #4 (pg 13)**
Camp Creepy Crawlers (smallest number is 1.0478)

**Conundrum #5 (pg 14)**
A. There are many possible combinations. Check to see that the combinations given actually do add up to $8800
B. yes—175 $50s; 2 $20s; 1 $10

**Conundrum #6 (pg 15)**

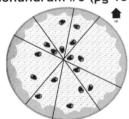

**Conundrum #7 (pg 16)**
Items that should be colored, falling on the line from left to right are: hamburger at (-4, -5); pizza slice at (-3, -3); container of popcorn at (-2, -1); doughnut at (-1, 1); hot dog at (1, 5)

**Conundrum #8 (pg 17)**
1400

**Conundrum #9 (pg 18)**
the number of broken toes in 10 weeks (15)

**Conundrum #10 (pg 19)**
Rosco

**Conundrum #11 (pg 20)**
A. 7 hours; B. 147 nautical miles

**Conundrum #12 (pg 21)**
0.5 in

**Conundrum #13 (pg 22)**
Missing number is 3 (consecutive integers are -3, -2, -1.)

**Conundrum #14 (pg 23)**
Estimate of measurement is 13cm$^2$

**Conundrum #15 (pg 24)**
10 combinations; 120 permutations

**Conundrum #16 (pg 25)**
A. 8:00 A.M.; B. 11:05 A.M.

**Conundrum #17 (pg 26)**
3/8 hour or 22 1/2 min

**Conundrum #18 (pg 27)**
Surface area = 216 in$^2$; 48 cubes were red on 2 sides

**Conundrum #19 (pg 28)**

**Conundrum #20 (pg 29)**
Archie was lying. Miles won the race.

**Conundrum #21 (pg 30)**
0.12 g

**Conundrum #22 (pg 31)**
Answers will vary. Student might choose RIGHT because it is the lowest ratio—so Meatball may think opponents LEAST expect this placement. OR,

CENTER might be the choice. It is the MOST used by Meatball, and thus his greatest skill. AND, they

might think that Meatball would expect them NOT to be prepared for his most frequent move. OR,

LEFT might be chosen. As the placement that is neither Meatball's most or least frequent, it could be argued that Meatball might choose that one to surprise the opponents.

**Conundrum #23 (pg 32)**

**Conundrum #24 (pg 33)**
Label the first student the instructor will count as #1. Rosco and friends should take positions #1, 2, 3, 4, 10, 11, 13, 14, 15, 17, 20, 21, 25, 28, and 29—moving clockwise around the circle.

**Conundrum #25 (pg 34)**
2/3; 1/324; probably c

**Conundrum #26 (pg 35)**
10% (Explanations will vary.)

**Conundrum #27 (pg 36)**

**Conundrum #28 (pg 37)**
24

**Conundrum #29 (pg 38)**
A. 0; B. (-25); C. (-42); D. ÷; E. 31

**Conundrum #30 (pg 39)**
All answers are 13 except for the question about the grape soda.

**Conundrum #31 (pg 40)**

8 to 1 score is not possible. There are many possible answers for the team scores. Check answers to see that they are reasonable.

**Conundrum #32 (pg 41)**

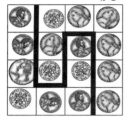

**Conundrum #33 (pg 42)**

Mercury or Mars

**Conundrum #34 (pg 43)**

Use the Pythagorean Theory to determine the distance between the point where Rosco entered the water and the point where he surfaced (6 feet) and add that to the original 7 feet. He comes up 13 feet away.

**Conundrum #35 (pg 44)**

**Conundrum #36 (pg 45)**

A. second
B. seven

**Conundrum #37 (pg 46)**

A. 1/2; B. 4/7; C. 5/7; D. 3/98

**Conundrum #38 (pg 47)**

A. 25
B. 9; Strategies will vary.

**Conundrum #39 (pg 48)**

There are many possible correct answers, e.g.: 34,901; 12,743; 10,943; 43,721; 16,703

**Conundrum #40 (pg 49)**

yes

**Conundrum #41 (pg 50)**

**Conundrum #42 (pg 51)**

Zion, IL: a lighted cigar; Sterling, CO: a tail light; Cresskill, NJ: wear three bells

**Conundrum #43 (pg 52)**

540

**Conundrum #44 (pg 53)**

4032

**Conundrum #45 (pg 54)**

A. Students might be able to show how 8 or 10 pans could fit; B. 1

**Conundrum #46 (pg 54)**

77

**Conundrum #47 (pg 55)**

A. 15 hours; B. 9 hours shorter (6 hours)

**Conundrum #48 (pg 57)**

1. 16; 2. 1848; 3. 5; 4. 10; 5. 5; 6. 336

**Conundrum #49 (pg 58)**

910 (Note: The total royalty available per song is 14% of $2.00 or 28 cents. So, for instance, on song 7, Rosco gets 2% of the $2 for being the producer, 3% of the $2 for being a co-writer with one other writer, and 2% for being a co-performer with the two other members of the band. This gives him a total of 7% of that $2.00)

**Conundrum #50 (pg 59)**

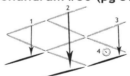

**Conundrum #51 (pg 60)**

A. Information not needed: the weight of the weights lifted on any of the machines, the number of repetitions on any of the machines, and the weight of the soda.
B. Information needed: Either the times that Rosco began and ended the entire workout (in which his rate of walking wouldn't matter) OR the distance he walked on the treadmill.

**Conundrum #52 (pg 61)**

The error is in the first step (the line below the problem). Solution is x = 12.

**Conundrum #53 (pg 62)**

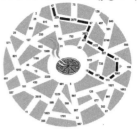

**Conundrum #54 (pg 63)**

66

**Conundrum #55 (pg 64)**

15

**Conundrum #56 (pg 65)**

36%

**Conundrum #57 (pg 66)**

140 ft; 5.4 mph

**Conundrum #58 (pg 67)**

360 cm

**Conundrum #59 (pg 68)**

Answers will vary, depending on the date. As of Dec 31, 2010: 780

**Conundrum #60 (pg 69)**

Reading across the next row: 1, 9, 36, 84, 126, 126, 84, 36, 9, 1; Reading across the last row: 1, 10, 45, 120, 210, 252, 210, 120, 45, 10, 1

**Conundrum #61 (pg 70)**

The flies Rosco swats have three distinct body parts, short antennae, and feet. He does NOT swat: B, C, E, G, H

**Conundrum #62 (pg 71)**

Rosco

**Conundrum #63 (pg 69)**

66

**Conundrum #64 (pg 69)**

Use equation b; The youngest cheese is one year old; oldest cheese is 22.

**Conundrum #65 (pg 69)**

1. (2, -5); 2. (3, 0); 3. (4, -5)

**Conundrum #66 (pg 69)**

Examples will vary.

**Conundrum #67 (pg 69)**

A. five; B. 96

**Conundrum #68 (pg 69)**

7600 ft. (Use the Pythagorean Theorem to find that the AB distance is 1200 ft.)

## Conundrum #69 (pg 78)
1. dots; 2. white; 3. white;
4. black; 5. white; 6. grey;
7. dots; 8. grey; 9. dots; 10. black

## Conundrum #70 (pg 79)
The cost pattern is: consonants
are worth 5, vowels are worth 2,
and numbers are worth 10. The
ranking, reading down the list is:
4, 2, 8, 1, 6, 3, 7, 5

## Conundrum #71 (pg 80)
Second recipe serves 75. Missing
number in first recipe is 3¾ C
shredded parmesan. Missing
amounts in second recipe: 1⅔ C
pepperoni; 12½ C sauce; 7½ T
basil; ⅚ C water.

## Conundrum #72 (pg 81)

a. 5-D;  b. 7-A;  c. 8-A;  d. 9-A;
e. 7-D;  f. 10-A;  g. 2-A;  h. 4-A;
i. 6-D;  j. 8-D;  k. 7-A;  l. 1-D;
m. 3-D;
Missing digits: from 1-Down: 2;
from 3-Down: 8; from 8-Across: 2

## Conundrum #73 (pg 82)
one on 42 and two on 82

## Conundrum #74 (pg 83)
A. 10:15 PM Tuesday
B. 6:45 PM Wednesday

## Conundrum #75 (pg 84)
A. 720; B. 360

## Conundrum #76 (pg 85)
yes (Suggestion: Use a string to
measure the ski trails, then
measure the string.)

## Conundrum #77 (pg 86)
Circle these: $3.626 \times 10^7$; $3.626 \times 10^8$; $2.1 \times 10^9$; $3.655 \times 10^8$; $1.1 \times 10^{10}$; and $1.01 \times 10^8$

## Conundrum #78 (pg 87)
Boomerang

## Conundrum #79 (pg 88)
$10.80

## Conundrum #80 (pg 89)
$1980 (1 KUL KAT, worth $10,020)
and (9LYVZ worth $8,040)

## Conundrum #81 (pg 90)
$247,500 per hour

## Conundrum #82 (pg 91)

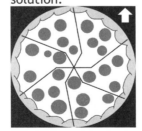

## Conundrum #83 (pg 92)
37 cm
(Note the position of the end
books. The front cover of the
first book is not on the outside
of the row. The back cover of
the last book is not on the
outside right end.)

## Conundrum #84 (pg 93)
A (1); B 5, 6); C 4

## Conundrum #85 (pg 94)
Frame 5: Score is 68;
Frame 7: Score is 98;
Frame 10: Score is 142

## Conundrum #86 (pg 95)
A (A: odds in favor are four to
eight or 1:2 and B odds against
are two to eight or 1:4)

## Conundrum #87 (pg 96)
Allow any solution that fulfills
instructions. Here is one
solution:

## Conundrum #88 (pg 97)
Every baby is a niece of Rosco.

## Conundrum #89 (pg 98)
A. 3/8; B. 1/4; C. 14/23; D.
2/23; E. 6/23

## Conundrum #90 (pg 99)
1 hr, 24 min.

## Show What You Know!
### Review and Assessment, pages 100-105
1. 120 (Number of permutations =
   5 x 4 x 3 x 2 x 1)
2. 15 (x + 1/3x + 2/3x + 12 + 12 +
   1/3x = 59)
3. 68 mph
4. b; Though the question does not
   ask for a solution to the problem,
   Sal is 6, Arlo is 3, Lucas is 1, and
   Rene is 4.
5. 210 minutes (or 3 1/2 hours)
6. a (the cone)
7. 40 cm
8. 10
9. Rosco
10. the sum of six times a number and
    the difference between negative
    twenty and twelve
11. $9x^2 \div (4)(5)$ (OR this can be written
    as a fraction with $9x^2$ as numerator
    and (4)(5) as denominator)
12. the number of times Boomerang
    asked Portia to dance
13. e
14. b
15. 14mph
16. 44 to 63 (or 44:63 or 44/63)
17. two
18. 9 (The cousins are 0, 3, 6, and 9.)
19. 24
20. e
21. d
22. P = 3/8
23. P = 7/20
24. P = 1/10
25. P = 33/40
26. a. 9:45 a.m.; b. Circle: *Rosco and
    his friends arrived halfway
    through the party to snap up
    scraps of food.*
27. a. 2/19; 2/9
28. e
29. 12 ft.
30. a
31. Boomerang
32. Cat #3
33. about 1,000 hours (200 min a day
    x 300 days divided by 60)
34. Ben; They jump in this order: Ren,
    Sven, Len, Jen, and Ben.
35. 12 pints
36. 24 in.$^3$
37. 10.8 miles
38. Arlo could have swatted 13, 14, or
    15.
39. 36 cm
40. 204